COUNSELING FOR CHURCH
VOCATIONS

But how are men to call upon him in whom they have not believed? And how are they to believe in him of whom they have never heard? And how are they to hear without a preacher? And how can men preach unless they are sent?

ROMANS 10:14–15, RSV

He who converts a soul draws water from a fountain; but he who trains a soulwinner, digs a well from which thousands may drink to eternal life.

CHARLES HADDON SPURGEON

COUNSELING
for
CHURCH VOCATIONS

Samuel Southard

BROADMAN PRESS
Nashville, Tennessee

Library of Congress Catalog Card Number: 57–8660
Printed in the United States of America
5.O56K.S.P.

To

Frances and Pamela

Introduction

Pastors can follow with profit the example of Professor Samuel Southard in their efforts to understand the crippling and destructive forces of existence and prevent these from blighting the lives of their people. Professor Southard spent much time and effort studying and ministering to the shattered lives of mentally ill persons. He served as a chaplain of the Central State Hospital in Kentucky for two years. He has already written a substantial volume on *The Family and Mental Illness*. However, the more he sought to solve the spiritual dilemmas of the acutely disturbed persons, the more insight he had as to the imperative necessity that every person have a meaningful, clear-cut, and richly informed sense of vocation in life. Consequently, he directed his graduate research toward understanding the counseling of candidates for church vocations. In the meantime, he worked for two more years in the intensive task of counseling and teaching theological students.

Therefore, the understanding and materials for the guidance of candidates for church vocations found in the following pages spring from deep personal experience, serious encounter with people who have lost the main meanings of their lives, and careful pastoral efforts to keep this from happening to others. Professor

Southard became intensely aware of the local pastor's possibilities in the spiritual guidance of aspirants toward full-time work in the church. He himself served in a brief but intensely meaningful pastorate. Much of the material in the following pages is a record of the results of that work.

Paradoxically enough, pastors in great numbers witness to the fact that they had little or no guidance as they set out on their pilgrimage as aspirants for the Christian ministry. Many tell of crippling blows and blocking impediments received from the hands that should have been most helpful, those of their pastors. Others give warm, grateful, and sustaining witness of the faithfulness and effectiveness of their pastors in counseling them through the years of their entry into, and preparation for, the Christian ministry. Yet, on the other hand, these men themselves may leave this counseling ministry to chance.

Professor Southard's book leads the way in clear, sound terms for the pastor or lay person who wants to put his heart into the pastoral care and counseling of the future leadership of our churches. I commend this book to the personal and painstaking study of every Christian pastor.

WAYNE E. OATES

Louisville, Kentucky

Contents

Contents

I
The Pastor's Opportunity

Every pastor covets some youth's choosing a church vocation under his ministry. Like the apostle Paul, he would like to discover his own "Timothy."

Great pastors have often considered their counseling on the special problems of a church vocation as one of the most significant parts of their personal ministry. Washington Gladden began to understand the value of serious conversations with students about lifework when he was a visiting preacher at Harvard. He enjoyed the daily personal contacts with his young counselees, many of whom had not made a vocational decision. Others wanted to talk about the best way to prepare for the work they had chosen.[1]

George Truett counseled young ministerial students of all denominations. He considered this one of the deepest and most abiding interests of all his efforts.[2]

The experienced pastor who shepherds a young person to life fulfilment in this high calling has doubled his own ministry.

An Unfulfilled Opportunity

Pastors, religious educators, and denominational workers have a unique opportunity in counseling young men and women who feel that their call to service is within a church-related institution. However, this opportunity is also a responsibility which many seminary students think is too often being poorly fulfilled. In 1954 the Department of Pastoral Psychology of the Southern Baptist Theological Seminary completed a two-year study which sought to determine something of the counseling which ministerial students receive. A questionnaire was distributed among the students at twenty seminaries of seven denominations.[3]

Fifteen hundred replies were received. In them, the students described the pastoral counseling they had received and made suggestions for improving their own future ministries in this area. The issues and conclusions of this book rest upon the experiences recounted by these fifteen hundred students. Here is personal information that should be helpful to every man with a shepherd's heart.

Again and again the students wrote that pastors did not meet the high expectations and deep needs of these eager "sons of the prophets." Although the average statement about the pastoral interview was favorable, there were many comments like the following:

I believe that with guidance and help I would have gone into the ministry during my high school days. At that time I thought I knew what I wanted to do, but after eight years in a machine shop and two years as a salesman, I answered God's call to my heart at the age of thirty-one.

I talked several times with men who should have been understanding and competent counselors, but who did not give the desired satisfaction of wise counsel. They gave advice of a subjective, negative nature when I was much in need of a positive sustaining attitude. My quest was to know God's call and to find out the requirements to fulfil that call.

The people who are devoting their lives to the ministry need more trained counseling than I've received. I feel that proper counseling could help me more than anything that could ever be taught in the classroom where the contact is so impersonal. Yet, I'm hesitant to ask for counseling because most people seem too busy and not interested in each other's problems.

This investigation points to one major conclusion: there is a great need for better counseling concerning church vocations. The students' answers pointed up strengths and weaknesses in pastoral counseling. This book will attempt to use these findings in two ways: to present the drama of thought and action through which young people move from first thoughts of a church vocation to the final stages of professional preparation, and to strengthen religious counselors in their work with these young people.

A word of caution is necessary, however. The comments and answers of the students indicate what they thought and remembered about counseling. No questionnaire can truly measure how any person feels. Emotions are deceiving and memories are unclear. Furthermore, any research into intangible spiritual factors is elusive. This book will offer some evidence that points in the direction of several general conclusions.

It does not attempt to give definite answers to the complex and sacred issues which revolve about the subject of church vocations.

Even when these limitations are accepted, a minister might still be doubtful of all this and say, "No one counseled me! I did not need any help. I was called of God and found my way into the ministry by myself fifty years ago." He may be right. Fifty years ago young men and women did not need all the personal guidance that is required in the complexities of youth's world today. Great changes have taken place.

The Need for Counsel

The first reason that young people need more counseling today is linked to a change in Protestant thinking. The complex forces of modern society have influenced both lay and clerical leadership to such an extent that church organization and administration now demand special training. Today theological seminaries are being supported even by denominations which were suspicious of an educated clergy in past generations. A pioneer in theological education of a hundred years ago saw the need of a trained ministry when he wrote:

I cannot bear that our preachers in Illinois and Missouri should continue as ignorant as some of them now are. In the three states are not less than 250 Baptist preachers. A majority of them have been raised on the frontiers, with scarcely the advantages of a common school education, and not even habituated to read the word of God in early life. Every year is adding to the number of this class of

4

preachers. . . . What should be done? Is not the path of duty plain as the noon-day sun? Furnish these men with the means of such education as circumstances admit. Establish a theological school.[4]

The second reason follows from the first: A complex church organization demands trained leadership. This means that the ministry is no longer just a "calling"; it is also a profession. Pastors often react against the term "profession" because it has come to imply a cold, impersonal, detached, and mechanical type of ministry. This use of "profession" designates a way of thinking which many ministers abhor.

But "profession" can also be used in a better sense, as in a description of the type of training received by a minister. When used in this way, it means instruction in many subjects that are all related to one profession, the ministry, and has as its goal the admonition of Paul to a young pastor: "Do your best to present yourself to God as one approved, a workman who has no need to be ashamed, rightly handling the word of truth" (2 Tim. 2:15) .[5]

Furthermore, it designates an independent way of thinking, an attitude of self-reliance, and an ability to handle with poise many different types of situations. When denominations decided that pastors, missionaries, and educational workers needed to receive an organized body of specialized knowledge before they would be proficient, the ministry became a profession as well as a calling.

A third indication of the need for counseling is suggested through the development of vocational counseling. This field gives a pastor useful information and techniques to help young people who are faced with the complexities of choosing a job in modern society. Ministers can no longer assume that there is just one choice which a young person can make when he feels called by God. Instead of just one task—preaching—there are at least forty-eight different specialties in church-related work. These are listed by John Oliver Nelson in *Opportunities in Protestant Religious Vocations.*

48.
specialties

Whether or not pastors agree with these premises, young people will still come to ministers when they are thinking about a church vocation. For every young person who does search out his pastor there are three others who want his counsel, according to the testimony of fifteen hundred students who had selected Christian vocations.

Not only did these young men want to talk to their pastors but they *did* talk to them more than they mentioned their thoughts to members of their families or to anyone else. Usually the young person, rather than the pastor, made the first step, especially among Episcopalians and Presbyterians. Among the Missouri Synod Lutherans the pastor most often took the initiative.

In Baptist churches the young people made their choice of church-related work public by coming to the front at the close of a church service. The pastor then announced their decisions to the church. In other com-

6

munions, the pastor announced these decisions as a part of a morning worship service, or names of those who had made such decisions were published in the church paper.

After making their vocational decisions, a majority of these young people sought out their pastors for counsel concerning the problems which confronted them. Yet, despite their desire to talk with their pastors, over two-thirds of the seminary students reported that they had to content themselves with a few informal contacts. How tragic this is! But many young people have deep affection for their ministers, like the student who wrote: "I went a hundred miles to see my former pastor who had been a childhood idol and who had been instrumental in leading me to Christ."

The Pastor's Responsibility

With this responsibility placed upon him by his young people, what are the pastor's responsibilities as a counselor concerning church vocations?

The first responsibility of the pastor, religious educator, or denominational worker is to act like a Christian in his relation to the young person who seeks his counsel. This advice may sound too obvious, but it is an important factor in a young person's decision. When young people admire and respect a pastor, they often identify with both his personality and his work. If this interest is heightened by their personal contacts with him, the pastor has followed the example of the apostle Paul, who told the Corinthians, "I became your father in Christ Jesus through the gospel. I urge you, then, be imitators of me" (1 Cor. 4:15–16) . A pastor is hardly following the apostolic example in his personal contacts when a seminary student can write a statement like this:

I was often rebuffed in attempting to counsel about my problems by the remark, "Just pray about it." It always seemed that my pastors were too busy, and I felt wrong about asking for their time when I was so young (nine years old) and so far away from my chosen field of service.

To act like a Christian means to young people that the minister will be interested in them as persons and will not take the disinterested attitude reported by one student: "As far as I am concerned, I had rather counsel with one in whom I had faith and who, I knew, had my interest at heart. There has never been this association between me and my pastor."

To act like a Christian also means that the pastor is interested in the whole personality of the individual. Young people want to talk about what their decision means in terms of their own understanding of God, their families, marriage, money, ambition, or personal worthiness. They do not wish to be treated like one student, who said, "I was just another statistic for the pastor to report at the associational meeting."

The pastor should also seek a religious interpretation of life, both in himself and in his young people. As Richard Baxter said, "The world is better able to read the nature of religion in a man's life than in the

Bible." [6] The religious counselor will therefore not only use prayer and the Bible in his counseling but will also seek the guidance of the Holy Spirit to direct his every thought and action in relation to those who seek his help.

All of these things seem obvious, but they are not. Ministers may think their counseling is religious, but students questioned in the 1954 study commented upon the lack of spiritual guidance from their pastors. Only 4 per cent of Southern Baptist pastors read any Scripture on God's call to men when students talked to them about a church vocation. Among other denominations, the highest percentage was 2 per cent, reported by the Presbyterians. The percentage of pastors who prayed with students about their decision ranged, in all seven denominations, from 25 per cent (Baptists) to 2 per cent (Episcopalians). After their first conversation, less than 10 per cent of the pastors in all seven denominations talked to the young men about their devotional life and the development of spiritual disciplines. One student summarized his own experience by saying: "My pastor-counselor's greatest failure lay in his lack of emphasis on the need of a consistent personal devotional life. A few practical and devotional books would have been helpful."

A second responsibility of the pastoral counselor is to help clarify a young person's vocational decision by placing it in the perspective of the universal Christian calling. The pastor or educational director is more than a vocational counselor. Young people come to him be-

9

cause of his training in theology and pastoral experience. As one student put it, "We need to understand the difference between commitment and commitment to this or that." Another said, "I thought ministers were experienced in what I wanted to know." Relating theological truths to human experience is a unique responsibility of the pastoral counselor.

Another responsibility of the counselor is related to the pastor's work as a representative of organized religion. People who are identified with a church vocation are expected to know their own denominational requirements for church work and to help young people understand their personal qualifications for such tasks. Concern about personal qualifications for a church vocation was one of the problems in making a vocational decision most frequently mentioned by the seminary students questioned. They consulted their pastors or a religious educator chiefly because of their expectation that they would understand the personal problems connected with their decision. In this area the pastors seemed to be most helpful. When asked how the counselor responded to their interest in a church vocation, students said that they were urged to get academic training and were helped to understand their decision. Students reported that as a result of the interview they had a stronger conviction of their call to a church vocation and were better able to evaluate their decision.

Pastors were not as helpful, however, in meeting a fourth responsibility, one which involves the need for factual information about church vocations, a description of the steps in preparation for such work, and suggestions of significant activities and devotions which would prepare the young person for such a vocation. In this area the pastors of only a fourth of the students were reported to bring even a minimum of help. Few young people were guided into church activities that would prepare them for a church vocation. A handful of students were given pamphlets or told to read specific books on a church vocation.

A final pastoral responsibility is to join with the young person in facing his personal problems and to share his struggles. The decision to answer a sacred calling usually presents as many dilemmas as it solves. These problems arise out of the readjustment of the young person's total sphere of family, social, and educational relationships because of his new concept of himself as a person dedicated to the work of God among men in the church. The pastor's function is to guide these creative concerns into the growing edge of the personality of the one who aspires to the work of God.

Out of fifteen hundred students questioned, only 11 per cent said that they were not conscious of any problem at the time of their decision for a church vocation. The majority went to their pastors because they could help with these problems, but only 6 per cent reported that they were helped with some intimate personal problem. As the young people progress from their home church to college to seminary, the need for counsel on personal matters increases. Furthermore, when adequate pastoral care is not available at the time that a problem first presents itself, the problem "snowballs" and attracts to itself other confusions. Thus the young person may present a chronic picture of maladjustment by the time he reaches the seminary. Candidates for church vocations need pastoral care and counseling at every stage in their vocational development.

The Student's Personality

A healthy personality is an indispensable prerequisite for service in a church vocation. A study of sixty ministerial students at Carthage College indicated that "good personality, its inward foundations in emotionality and its external applications in social relations, seems to be the one all-important necessity." [7] Fifty-two veteran missionaries interviewed by Robert Oberly stressed "ability to get along with people" as a prerequisite for missionary service.

Since pastoral counseling on personal problems is of such great importance in developing a healthy personality dedicated to God's service, later chapters will present some of the common problems of candidates for a church vocation and some suggestions for meeting them. The task of guiding those who choose this work is weighty. But every pastor who fulfils that responsibility has seen this Scripture come alive:

And his gifts were that some should be apostles, some prophets, some evangelists, some pastors and teachers, for the equipment of the saints, for the work of ministry, for building up the body of Christ, until we all attain to the unity of the faith and of the knowledge of the Son of God, to mature manhood, to the measure of the stature of the fullness of Christ; so that we may no longer be children, tossed to and fro and carried about with every wind of doctrine, by the cunning of men, by their craftiness in deceitful wiles. Rather, speaking the truth in love, we are to grow up in every way into him who is the head, into Christ, from whom the whole body, joined and knit together by every joint with which it is supplied, when each part is working properly, makes bodily growth and upbuilds itself in love (Eph. 4:11–16).

II

Signs of Interest in
a Church Vocation

A long time is usually required for young people to make definite a decision to enter a church-centered profession. Many problems arise. Some of them are solved alone. Some require the pastor's assistance.

Jesus said, "He who has ears to hear, let him hear" (Matt. 11:15). Pastors should have ears attuned to hear the problems of their people. But often the still small voices in the wilderness of decision are drowned in the noisy preoccupations of other matters that beset the pastor. Pastors may have eyes and still be befogged to human need. There are signs and sounds which will alert the pastor to the fact that a young person has talent and motivation toward a church vocation.

Childhood

One of the first signs of interest occurs when a child joins the church. Summer Bible conferences often make a dual appeal for children to confess faith in Christ and dedicate themselves to "full-time Christian service." An eleven-year-old girl, Ann, returned from such a conference and told her pastor, Mr. Delta, that she had "given her heart to Jesus" at camp and wanted to join the church. In talking with her parents, the pastor found that she had also gone forward during the dedication service. As Mr. Delta talked to her before she joined the church, Ann said, "I want to join the church so that everyone will know that I belong to Jesus." When he asked about her interest in religious work, she said, "I don't think about any particular church work. I just want to work for Jesus." The pastor did not try to force her into a definite vocational decision. Instead, he pointed out that her efforts to bring a friend next door to church would be an example of Christian service. "Oh, yes," she said, "I want Mary to make Jesus her Saviour, too. I talk to her about it, but her parents want her to wait. I'll keep trying."

In this instance, Ann demonstrated good understanding of what it means to join the church. Furthermore, she was actively working to bring others to Christ. Although her vocational ambitions were naturally vague, Mr. Delta saw a good foundation of interest upon which he might build, in years to come, either toward a church vocation or toward a lay vocation dedicated to Christian ideals.

As a contrast to this solid foundation, another girl of the same age went forward during the same dedication service. Later she told her pastor that she "had definitely decided to be a foreign missionary." Unfortunately, this young lady had much difficulty getting along with other people her own age. One of the primary qualifications for mission service is an ability to work with people. Furthermore, her mother had talked several times to the pastor about the grade school principal's "accusations" that her daughter was "a retarded child." Here the pastor had an obligation to both the girl and the church to lead her toward some work for which she was actually qualified. There are many honorable and productive positions for persons of below-normal intelligence, but a missionary appointment which requires college and seminary education is not one of them.

Children may also show interest in a church vocation in "pastor's classes" studying church membership. James, a twelve-year-old boy, impressed his pastor with his biblical knowledge in such a class. He also thought through theological questions, such as the following:

PASTOR: What does it mean to testify for Jesus?
JAMES: You mean, like testimony in a criminal court?
PASTOR: In one way.
JAMES: You mean, testimony for the defendant?
PASTOR: Yes.
JAMES: And in this case the defendant is Jesus and we are the witnesses for him.
PASTOR: That's right.
JAMES: Then I would say that to testify for Jesus means to stand up for him whenever he is on trial with your buddies or anybody else.

Here was the dawning awareness of the intention of God. This conversation demonstrated James' ability to relate religion to life and his willingness to ask questions when he needed information. Here is excellent ground in which the yearnings for a divine mission may grow. Later the pastor saw confirmation of this early promise when James was elected president of a teen-age Bible study group. He took full control of the program, called all those who had parts on the program, saw that his room was in order, and reported his successes to the pastor. The seed was beginning to bear fruit.

In childhood the signs of a growing sense of a Christian vocation are an interest in the conversion of friends, a clear understanding of the meaning of church membership—which shows much thought beforehand, an inquiring mind about religion, and an enthusiastic leadership in church work. The counselor will find that these signs are guides for his work.

Adolescence

As the young person moves into early adolescence, the same guideposts remain, although they should naturally be more mature signs. Further, the beginning of boy-girl problems complicates the issues.

Albert, a fourteen-year-old boy, demonstrated a more mature interest when he told his father that he wished to dedicate his life to work in his denomination. The father was alarmed and told the pastor that the boy should not come to church so much because "he's getting too preoccupied with religion." When the pastor invited the boy to visit him, he found no morbid preoccupation. Instead, Albert was concerned about a friend whose father had just died. "I don't know

17

how to help him," said Albert, "but I know that he's hurt. What does death really mean?"

After a discussion of the resurrection, Albert said he thought everyone had some questions like that, and he wanted to help answer them. The pastor suggested that he begin to "draw out" his friends and come to the pastor if there were questions that he could not answer. "That appeals to me," said the boy. "I've been looking for something to do for God, and this seems to be the answer."

Albert had a healthy interest in religious topics, sensitivity to the needs of others, and a desire to help them with the Christian answers. These are good signs that may lead to a fruitful ministry. However, the pastor must, in the future, look carefully at this boy's relation to his father. He does not know at this time whether or not Albert does occasionally become morbid and depressed about religion. Perhaps the father has a problem with religion which he is reading into his son's normal interest, or the conflict may come from other difficulties within these persons' hearts.

Boy-girl relationships absorb teen-agers and certainly influence every area of their thinking, including thoughts about religion. They may feel guilty about their sexual habits or alarmed by the strange new passions which surge up in them. Teen-agers, as well as others, may think that church work is a "safe" vocation in which people are untroubled by the turbulent emotions which are normal to red-blooded young people. Or they may "dedicate their lives" to seek to atone for "sinful" thoughts or deeds. On the other hand, a sense of guilt may make them feel unworthy of a church vocation and for years may cast a cloud over their God-given motivations.

In such a situation as this, the minister may be the only understanding adult to whom teen-agers will turn. If he is alert to their problems, they may be able to distinguish between religion as a way of handling adolescent conflicts and religion as a life-time vocational choice.

The pastor does not need to go to the extremes of some psychoanalysts who say that *any* guilt means that *all* choices and acts for the rest of life have an unresolved sexual conflict as their base. The fact of the matter is that young men and women enter a church vocation for any number of reasons, some worthy, some less worthy. The challenge to the pastor is to take that motivation as it is and mold it under God's spirit into a stable, realistic life dedication. As thoughtful seminary professors say, "We are not interested so much in why they came here as we are in what they become by the time they leave here."

For example, a young man who had dedicated himself to a church vocation sought the help of a prominent denominational leader about some theological doubts. The preacher said harshly and quickly, "No man called of God doubts anything. You are guilty of either drinking or adultery." Since the young man had done neither, he began to look back into his life for some earlier sin. He remembered his struggles with sexual fantasies

19

both before and after his decision for a church vocation at the age of fifteen. He concluded that guilt feelings drove him into the ministry. Not until he had talked several times with another minister, a patient pastor with a shepherd's heart and skill, did he regain his sense of balance and see that he had solved this struggle when he found acceptance in college youth groups. His earlier thoughts were bred in loneliness. When he was around people of his own age, his natural friendliness expanded and replaced morbid thoughts. It was this friendliness and love for people on which his dedication to the ministry could be built for the future.

In early adolescence, therefore, the counseling pastor should look for more mature and deeper questions about life, active church service, and the stresses relating to the opposite sex. Help with the transient problems of that age will equip the young person for a clear vocational decision. A passage of Scripture that speaks of this tension between sex and vocation is 1 Corinthians 7:32–35:

I want you to be free from anxieties. The unmarried man is anxious about the affairs of the Lord, how to please the Lord; but the married man is anxious about worldly affairs, how to please his wife, and his interests are divided. And the unmarried woman or girl is anxious about the affairs of the Lord, how to be holy in body and spirit; but the married woman is anxious about worldly affairs, how to please her husband. I say this for your own benefit, not to lay any restraint upon you, but to promote good order and to secure your undivided devotion to the Lord.

The questions put to the Corinthians by Paul could equally well be heard in a pastor's study. If a seventeen-year-old girl has publicly stated her decision for a church vocation, how will this alter her conduct? Will she date the same boys, or must she look only for one who is going to enter the ministry? Perhaps she is confused as to whether she should date at all, for no one may have told her how marriage and vocation can be combined. She may even assume that her decision makes her an unofficial nun who would lose God's approval and renounce his call if she were to fall in love and marry.

Ministers can point out to young women that in the seminaries of some denominations the relation between vocation and marriage is very close. Unmarried women who major in Christian education devote many hours to the care of children. They may work with women who are married to theological students, and in a seminary nursery both will be giving thought to the ways in which the rearing of children affects the parents' church vocation, and vice versa. Instead of being divorced from marriage, unmarried women can receive in a church vocation such training as will fit them for significant service to the Christian family.

A similar emphasis can be made with young men. One of the stronger temptations may be for them to assume that their vocational decision has made them the divine exception in courtship, marriage, and the family. The words of Paul may be interpreted by some Protestants, as well as by some Catholics, to mean free-

21

dom from family responsibility. As a result, a young man may place his vocation and his dating in separate compartments of his mind if no one has shown him the intimate connection between the way he behaves on Saturday night and the way he preaches on Sunday morning. Reverence for personality should be the guiding principle in all his relationships.

Furthermore, the temptation to separate marriage and religion may cause a minister to continue to ignore the needs of a wife for affection, help with the housework, and an occasional dinner downtown. The "Lord's work" may be thought of only in relation to *his* day, *his* book, *his* man. But 1 Corinthians 7:36–38 discusses marriage as a religious decision. It is contradictory for a theological student to study about Christian ethics all day and assume that his wife should wait on him all evening.

The tragic fruit of a split between sex and vocation is seen in the neglect of children, whether it be in the one-room apartments of theological students or in a too-roomy parsonage. The bitter comments which some sons of ministers make about their fathers and their fathers' church work demand some serious study of the relation between a minister's work and his family. Such a study has not yet been made.

Later Youth

Most seminary students made their decision for the ministry between the ages of seventeen and twenty-four. There has not been any definite study on the signs which can guide a pastor at this important time in a vocational decision. However, a few things can be noted here with the hope that ministers will be dissatisfied enough to write their own conclusions.

An independent decision, made prayerfully with God's guidance, is the first sign. The young person makes this choice by himself. As one divinity student wrote:

> I do not wish to seem overly pious or spiritual, but I have always been inclined to take all of my problems, or anything that called for a decision, to God. I have received help from personal friends, but I consider this as part of God's directing. Every struggle that I undergo is always in his presence—prayer has been a most vital element in all of my Christian experience.

Although the youth may talk about the influence of parents, pastor, or others on the decision, the counselor to whom he confides this solitary decision must recognize and acknowledge that note of independence, that sentiment which leads this young person to stand alone like Martin Luther and say, "God helping me, I can do no other." But the pastor must also note carefully how the person approaches him about this decision.

Another indication of genuine interest comes when the young person seeks out the pastor or some other professional religious worker to talk about a church vocation. Most of the seminary students who were questioned in 1954 had sought factual information and some clarification of their vocational decision. They should be able to obtain this help from their ministers. If a young person tells everyone except his pastor or another religious worker, then something is wrong —either with the pastor or with the young person's decision.

One ministerial candidate emphasized the need for a pastor's help when he wrote:

These words may seem contradictory because of my confidence in and love of my pastor. He was helpful, but as I look back his help was inadequate. Personal counseling with someone perhaps would have made the way easier for me in that he could have given more guidance. I was not aware of how much the informal chats helped me as I dropped by his home on Saturday night. But it has had more effect than I realized.

On the other hand, if a young person is uncertain, he often will not consult his pastor. One young man wrote to his family that he was entering the ministry, but when he came home from a summer camp he did not even acknowledge the letter his pastor wrote him about a church vocation. However, he continued to talk about being an evangelist. One of the other young people laughingly told the pastor, "Jim tells everybody he knows about it, but he always tells them it is a secret. He says he's not ready to proclaim it openly because it's too big a thing. Actually, I don't think he knows what he's talking about." When the pastor said that he wondered why Jim had not talked over his decision with him, the young man replied, "I figure Jim is scared to talk to anyone who really knows what religion is all about. He's just playing around with this."

Obviously the pastor must guard against taking the opinion of Jim's contemporaries at face value. Jim may really have a concern for evangelism. But it is significant that he does not come to the person with whom he would logically want to talk. What blocks communication between these two?

A third sign of interest in a church vocation is the willingness of the young person to work with other young people in student Christian organizations at school or in the church. Many seminary students spoke of the great help of these organizations in feeling at ease with people. Since one of the primary requirements of a church vocation is an ability to get along with people, the pastor will be very alert to this trait in those who talk about a church vocation.

It is important to distinguish between what a young person *says* about his interest in people and how he *acts* and *feels* with others. For example, a young lady told her pastor that she wanted to witness every day to friends and go into religious work. "I just love to talk to people about religion," she said. However, when the pastor led a young people's summer retreat, he found that this girl loved to *argue* with people about *her* version of religion. She was constantly defending the Bible against the questions of others; yet when she tried to demonstrate biblical knowledge, she herself made many errors. Her contemporaries interpreted her attitude as arrogance and an attempt to use religion to dominate them.

The pastor spoke to her quietly about her interest in religion and said, "You like to read the Bible, I take it, but have difficulty finding the right passages to answer questions. Would you like some help in getting the right information?" The girl said that she needed all the help she could get, for she felt lonely and afraid in her group. The manner of the pastor reassured her. She began to pay attention to her dress, spoke cheerfully to others, and, under the pastor's coaching, began to ask others for their opinions. She began to be a very likable person.

By sensing her social isolation, the pastor was able to help her to express her religious interest in a positive way. Instead of using the Bible to defend herself and *talking* about an interest in people, she responded to the pastor's interest by showing a genuine warmth, which flowed over into her relations with other young people. Such a person will need careful coaching, on occasion, for a long time, but a beginning has been made.

In addition to these indications of healthy motivation toward the ministry, there are also the objective qualifications of the minister set forth in 1 Timothy 3:1-7. A discussion of these may be found on pages 43-60 of *The Christian Pastor* by Wayne Oates. Furthermore, a handy self-analysis for ministers containing a check list on physique and personal appearance, mental, temperamental, and social qualities, religious life, and financial relations is found in chapter 9 of *The Minister's Job* by Albert Palmer.

But the three "signs" mentioned above are still all important, because they deal with the person's relation to God and to men. George Arbaugh concluded a study of sixty ministerial students by writing:

> The most striking thing about these findings is that the four traits which seem to be most greatly stressed in theological education have least to do with success or failure, viz., theological understanding, religious information, intelligence, and scholarship. Good personality, its inward foundations in emotionality and its external applications in social relations, seems to be the one all-important necessity.[1]

Adulthood

The 1954 study revealed that vocational choice came between the ages of seventeen and twenty-two among Baptists. It tended to be a year or two later among Methodists and Presbyterians, and about four years later among Episcopalians. About 20 per cent of the fifteen hundred students studied made their decision between twenty-three and fifty-one. Sixteen per cent of the Episcopalians made the decision between twenty-nine and thirty-five. Among Baptists and Methodists who do not attend a seminary the number of older men entering the ministry may be high. No study of students in college religion departments or Bible schools is available.

There is one sign of a healthy adult dedication to

27

a church vocation which may be stressed here. The call creates as many problems as it solves. This statement is true at any time, but it becomes especially important in adulthood when men must leave established jobs, sell their homes, and provide for their families. One older seminary student wrote:

I did not have a competent person to help me, and I struggled through some experiences and decisions that I doubt I could make alone again. I had three children, had been out of school ten years. Had never attended college. Had to sell my home, farm, and start life over in a new direction. These were tremendous problems alone. I would have appreciated a pastor or some trained person to help me, but there were none.

Almost a third of the fifteen hundred students studied were working at the time they decided for a church vocation. An exceptionally large number of Episcopalians (15 per cent) were in professional work, while the total of 6 per cent in professional work among the fifteen hundred is close to the national average of 5.3 per cent. It is foolish to say that a man should enter the ministry if he can't do anything else, since over a third of these seminary students *did* something else, and giving up jobs they liked was a problem to half of those who were working. Here is the story of a student who was successful in both the church and his profession:

I was an accountant in secular work, served my church three years as a Sunday school superintendent. I casually

28

remarked to pastor on one occasion I thought I would like full-time religious work. Several weeks later, unknown to me, my pastor, after consultation with the deacons, recommended that the church employ me as full-time religious education director. I was approached by the pastor and deacons on the matter before presentation to the church. After much inner conflict, I was convinced God wanted me to accept. I was called by the church. I served three and one-half years and decided I needed training in the seminary. I sold my home and came to the seminary. This was a difficult decision since I have a wife and three children. I have been in the seminary since September, and am convinced I am just where God wants me for this present time. From here—that is up to the Lord.

Since only 11 per cent of the whole group of students said they were aware of no problems when they made their decisions to enter the ministry, and since these problems increase with age, it is usually true that older men will talk these matters over seriously with their pastor.

But what if an older man stoutly maintains that he has no problem? Here is a time for the pastor to look carefully into this man's background. What problem is he trying to solve by going into the ministry?

The pastor of a downtown city church faced this question when a thirty-two-year-old man called to say that he had heard "God's call." "Everything is perfect between the Lord and me," he said, "and I'm ready to leave home and preach any time." The pastor heard this reference to leaving home and said, "Just how are things at home?" The man replied, "Well, since you mention it, my marriage is about on the rocks. But I knew there was something better for me. The Lord will provide. I told my wife that if she couldn't forget what gossipy people said about me, I would show what a husband should be. I'd be a minister."

Further questioning revealed that the man had been "stepping out" with a city girl while his wife remained in a near-by village with their two children. When a fellow worker in his plant spread the news, the wife threatened to leave. In a panic, the husband had said, "I'm going to do right. From now on everything will be perfect. I'll be a preacher." The pastor urged him to come in with his wife to discuss their marriage before he went any further toward a vocational change. The man promised to do so but never returned.

The obvious failure of this man's marriage led him to seek the ministry as his refuge from guilt and social punishment. He thought that a "call to preach" would solve everything.

At times this insistence that all problems are solved magically by God is a sign of mental disturbance. God does give men power to work through their problems to spiritual victory. This, however, is not the same as the psychotic delusion that God will magically change all reality to suit the convenience of a mentally sick person.

When a person appears in the pastor's study with a sudden pronouncement that he has a "divine commission," it is well to ask about this person's previous religious experience. The person may be suffering from an acute mental illness. Paul warned Timothy against accepting "new converts" into the ministry (1 Tim. 3:6). The following example will show why that is still good advice:

Pastor McMan was surprised when John C., who had just joined the church after years of drunkenness and wife-beating, arose in a prayer meeting to say that he had personally won hundreds of persons to the Lord. The entire congregation was shocked several weeks later when John called on a dying saint of the church and said, "I have a message from the Lord. You will be dead by morning. Listen to me, for I have won a thousand men to Christ. You are a sinner. Obey me and you will live." When the saint died that night, sentiment became so strong that John stayed away from church. However, he called on the minister to announce that he would soon take over the pulpit and denounce the sinners who opposed him.

The pastor called John's wife, who was almost hysterical because John had threatened to kill her the night before for "opposing the Lord's will." The pastor advised her to call a psychiatrist. When John refused to see him, she had him arrested and sent to a state mental hospital.

At the hospital, John told the chaplains that he was Christ's eldest brother. The number of persons saved had risen to over two thousand. "I have saved more people than any preacher in the world." Neither electric shock treatment nor religious counsel dislodged his fixed delusional system.

In this instance, the sickness was so evident that the pastor and church did not fall into the snare of exalting —and ordaining—this man before he had time to prove his faith by works, by the corporate acceptance of the fellowship of believers, and by a demonstration of his own emotional stability.

Both of these examples show abnormal preoccupation with personal problems rather than a realistic concern for the people to be served by a pastor. The "call" was the final answer, the magic formula to help these men hide from past failures and overwhelming guilt. They called upon God to erase unconfessed sin and blind men to their personal inadequacies, instead of praying for forgiveness, self-understanding, and strength to face the future. Their disdain for themselves and others was twisted into a sense of omnipotence and perfection which protected them from reality. This is the very opposite of the biblical view of a call from God found in Isaiah 6 or Romans 10.[2]

This generalization, that the adult decision for a church vocation creates problems instead of magically solving them, may also be applied to some of the moral dilemmas facing men who wish to enter the ministry. All ministers have experienced some failure, but the sheltered background of some pastoral counselors has prevented them from entering into the sufferings of those who hate a brutal father, who have repented of an unwise marriage, or who have schemed—and been convicted—in the vicious competitive practices of a secular business world. Any of these may rise up to plague an older man with doubts about his decision to enter a church vocation.

Especially grievous is the problem of the divorced person who decides for a church vocation after he is separated from the marital partner. There has been no research on this question, although Professor Seward Hiltner of Chicago is now gathering material from the histories of divorced ministers. In the absence of reliable, organized evidence, pastors and theological professors use the best judgment they have: the memory of a similar case, ecclesiology, the system of ethics they were taught, community opinion, and their own personal inclinations.

It would be well for pastors to reserve judgment until they see how the problem of divorce motivates the person's decision for a church vocation. Does he say, "I must atone for this failure by dedicating my life to God?" This is not a sound foundation for a decision—whether the failure is divorce or something else. Giving up one's body to be burned without love is nothing, said Paul (1 Cor. 13:3). In desperation men may try to *be* good by works when they despair of *becoming* acceptable in their hearts before God. Unless such persons come to believe that God accepts them upon confession as they *are,* all they *do* will not restore their souls.

On the other hand, the parishioner may say, "I was divorced two years ago. There were mistakes on both sides. It's over, but I know it could affect my ministry. I'll be glad to tell you anything about it that might be helpful in setting things right for my future career." Here the person is open about his failure. He has handled it, yet knows there are pitfalls to be avoided because of it. With this type of understanding, real pastoral counseling can begin. With the problem in the open, the pastor can at least face realistically with the divorced person the limitations and hardships he will face in future employment. The acute social pressure of a strict church on a divorced minister places added strain on whatever emotional health he has. Can he take it?

Another difficulty is that of the person who has received psychiatric treatment. Since estimates of the number of persons who will receive such treatment during a lifetime run from one in five to one in ten, the pastor will probably meet several persons who make the decision for a church vocation after psychiatric treatment.

One of the important things to consider is how the former illness is related to the present decision. The thirty-two-year-old schoolteacher who tells her pastor that she wishes to enter religious educational work may reveal the fact of hospitalization for emotional depression when she was eighteen years old. But if she has had no severe "blue spells" in the past fourteen years, she may actually be a more sensitive and healthy person as a result of her treatment. On the other hand, a forty-year-old man who has been chronically dissatisfied in several jobs despite year-long psychiatric interviews may reveal that he is seeking work as an assistant pastor or educational director because he should find less exacting employment. The church has suffered too much with this low estimate of church work to permit such a person's views to go unchallenged.

FIRST PRESBYTERIAN CHURCH

ANNOUNCES ITS ELEVENTH SERIES OF SERMONS FOR FEBRUARY

11:00 A. M.
CHARACTER STUDIES IN O. T.

February 3—JACOB
February 10—JOB
February 17—ABRAHAM
February 24—JONAH
(Broadcast WMAP)

7:00 P. M.
SERMONS FOR HOME-MAKERS

Feb. 3—Motion Picture:
"Are You Ready For Marriage?"
Feb. 10—"Are You In Love?"
Feb. 17—"Young People In History"
T. C. Dove, Jr.
Feb. 24—"The Ideal Marriage"

SPECIAL MUSIC EACH EVENING

When men have a genuine experience of God's grace despite their failures, they need the restorative power of a Christian fellowship, like the student who wrote:

Before I became a Christian I had lived very haphazardly. I did not have a high school education and had thought very little about anything. When I became a Christian I felt very insecure and unworthy and had only a few informal conferences because of an inferior feeling. Perhaps a good conference would do me good and help straighten out my mind and thoughts.

As pastors counsel with souls struggling to affirm God's claim upon their incomplete lives, they may well remember the words of an outstanding minister, who said:

Sometimes I think we preachers, overawed by the formal dignity of the pulpit, talk too anonymously and impersonally. Here I am today, an older man talking to you about the secret of spiritual power in general, when all the time what I am really seeing in my imagination's eye is that young man I was years ago, shot all to pieces, done in and shattered in a nervous breakdown, foolishly undertaking too much work and doing it unwisely, all my hopes in ashes and life towering over me, saying, you are finished; you cannot; you are done for. People ask me why in young manhood I wrote *The Meaning of Prayer*. That came out of young manhood's struggle. I desperately needed a second chance and reinforcement to carry on with it. I was sunk unless I could find at least a little of what Paul had in mind when he said, I can—"In Him who strengthens me, I am able for anything." [3]

III
A Case Study

Any counseling done by a minister in his role as a pastor is pastoral counseling. Ministers are not marriage and family counselors one hour and vocational counselors the next. The pastor considers all the varied needs of his people, some of which deal with the choice of a life mate, some with the choice of a life's work.

In this chapter an actual example of pastoral counseling will be considered and conclusions drawn from it. A pastor's reaching conclusions on the basis of his own experience is more creative than relying on someone else to draw up quick and easy rules to follow in all cases. This chapter is meant to encourage such thinking.

An emphasis on systematic evaluation of his own experience points up one thing: the pastor should write summaries of his interviews. Only unmarried preachers can ever claim infallible memories! Married men who try to remember what their wives have told them to bring home from the store after their pastoral calls have learned to take to pad and pencil long ago.

So with interviews. Immediately after the conference, the minister can jot down on his "memo" book important impressions. At night as he reviews the day's work, he can write out a paragraph on typing paper and file it in a Manila folder under the person's name. Interested pastors will find a discussion on keeping records in the last chapter of *The Minister's Consultation Clinic.*

Pastor Sheraton's Counseling

One pastor, Mr. Sheraton, recorded his interviews concerning a church vocation with one of his young people, Joe, an eighteen-year-old high school senior. Joe first asked what a man could do in Vacation Bible school. The pastor replied that he could help with the handwork. Joe did so, but afterwards told the pastor that he was disappointed because he had no real opportunity to talk with the boys about religion, since this was all done by women in classes. Mr. Sheraton realized his mistake and asked Joe if he were seriously interested in full-time religious work. Joe thought he was.

The principle suggested here is that young people are eager to explore the inside of a vocation. The pastor has a responsibility to lead them to the very heart of it. Instead of making Joe a part of the teaching staff, Mr. Sheraton unwittingly shoved him to the side. He had considered the organizational needs of the church without paying close attention to the unspoken needs of this young man.

Several months later Joe said that he would like to go visiting with Mr. Sheraton. Since it was almost time for college, they could not find an opportunity, but the pastor did give Joe several booklets about church work and asked Joe to come in and discuss them with him.

Mr. Sheraton might have *made* time to visit with Joe. However, he did one good thing. If a person is definitely interested, specific literature is very helpful. It saves time, gives accurate information, and gauges the person's actual interest. Those who are only superficially interested will not bother to read much. Those who hunger for information will appreciate all they are given. It is good to have on hand graded literature from promotional pamphlets to classics on the pastoral office—and to give them out in that order. Chapter five of this book offers suggestions for the pastor's bookshelf.

Joe returned the books just before leaving for college and said they were very helpful. At Thanksgiving the pastor visited a near-by college and invited Joe over for dinner with other students from the church. Joe came and talked of his enthusiasm for college work. However, he was concerned about the ways of living he found in his dormitory.

Here is another lesson for the pastor. He can pay attention to people when they *do not* have any problems. In this way he reassures the flock that the shepherd loves them for what they are rather than for the interesting experiences which they describe to him. Mr. Sheraton showed an interest in Joe as a college student whether or not he entered a church vocation.

At Christmas Joe came by the parsonage to ask a question about the book of Romans. After a brief explanation, Mr. Sheraton asked why he was interested.

Joe replied that he was looking for some help on God's call to men and hadn't found any satisfactory explanation yet. The pastor discussed the theology of a "call" and then asked Joe to read Isaiah 6 and report his thoughts on the matter.

Several comments may be made about this interview. First, when a person displays religious interest, it is wise to ask why he does so. If this is done with Christian courtesy, people appreciate this notice of their religious thinking and usually are encouraged to go deeper into their own private world for an explanation. Second, when Joe asked for religious information, Mr. Sheraton gave it to him. This was not the time to say, "How do you feel about it?" That could come later.

The third basic procedure is to give the person a specific assignment and ask him to report his own views. Then will be the time to ask how he "feels" about the call. Without adequate information, the counselee will be probing in the dark.

On the following Sunday Mr. Sheraton preached on "What is a Religious Experience?" with Isaiah 6 as the text. As Joe left the church he said, "Thanks for the help. That answers many questions."

The sermon was not "aimed" at Joe but was designed to answer some of his questions. Pastoral counselors have opportunity to deal with a wide range of questions from an absolute authority, the Bible, Sunday by Sunday in their sermons. Often when a pastor feels a lecture coming on during counseling, he may discover that it is the budding outline of next week's sermon. It should be given much more attention in the study rather than being prematurely exposed to the heat of discussion. The pastor who is an attentive listener will often have people say, "Why, you haven't said anything!" To which the pastor may reply, "I'm satisfied to listen to your thoughts. I get to talk without interruption each Sunday."

Spring vacation brought Joe home in time for prayer meeting. He asked to see Mr. Sheraton afterwards. As they sat down in the church study, the boy began the conversation.

JOE: I can't fight this thing any longer. I want to become a minister.

PASTOR: How has your family taken this, Joe?

JOE: Ah, my dad says I should make my own decision. He's swell about it. (*Pause*.)

PASTOR: And your mother?

JOE: Oh, she wanted me to go into engineering. She's always wanted me to be successful like my grandfather, she says. I'm afraid she thinks I don't quite know my own mind.

PASTOR: Well?

JOE: That's a good point. In some ways I'm sure, but there are lots of things about engineering, like the pay and the position and—well, we have never had any ministers in our family, and—it's just that nobody in my family thinks like a preacher, if you know what I mean.

PASTOR: You mean that they don't understand the kind of world of which you would be a part as a minister?

JOE: That's it. Don't get me wrong: my family is swell,

but they never thought of me as being that religious. They're not religious athletes, you know, bounding from one church service to another.

PASTOR: Yes, I know. Now how is this going to affect your work as a minister?

JOE: I think it'll help. I know so many—well, let's say some preachers who don't seem to understand what ordinary people are like. I've lived in a "worldly" world. I know how they think, what they do. I think I know how to speak their language and appeal to them.

PASTOR: Sounds good. How would you appeal to them?

JOE: Well, take my mother for example. She would really get her back up at any "holier-than-thou" appeal. But when I say, "O.K., I won't make $10,000 a year, but I'll be doing the thing I really want to do," then she takes it easier.

At this point the choir director opened the door and asked the sermon topics for Sunday so that hymns could be selected and rehearsed by the choir. Joe got up to leave.

JOE: I won't take any more of your time now. Thanks for your help.

PASTOR: Are you far enough along in your thinking to make this decision public?

JOE: Well, a little later, yes.

A quick glance at this interview tells several things about Joe. He had made up his mind after thinking about this decision for almost a year. It was definite enough for him to tell his parents. He had some problem with his mother but was handling it himself. He was not yet far enough along in his thinking to go into details about the training and work of a minister or to make his decision public.

Several things are also revealed about Mr. Sheraton. The fact that Joe spoke of himself so freely shows that the pastor kept himself in the background. However, Mr. Sheraton was not passive. He guided the interview to a discussion of such an essential point as the parents' reactions. He stayed with this idea until Joe spoke about the problem he had with his mother. The pastor pointed out the possible relation of this difficulty to his future ministry and let Joe explain it. Finally, the counselor moved toward a definite commitment.

In general it can be said that Mr. Sheraton tried to be alert to Joe's personal concerns. All the while he kept the interview centered on the major objective of Joe's visit—the decision for a church vocation. He did not push the young man into a quick public announcement, since Joe may still have some things to talk over and live through with his mother and has not gone very deeply into the practical details of the ministry. Furthermore, although he talked several months before of being helped by a sermon on religious experience, Joe has not told his personal religious experience with God concerning a church vocation.

Why did Mr. Sheraton not pray with Joe about this decision? Did the interruption distract them or cause the pastor to feel that prayer would be "tacked on" after the spirit of the hour was broken? The reason in this case is not known, but it is known that only 14 per cent of fifteen hundred seminary students said that their pastor recommended prayer at the time of their definite decision. The majority of these were Baptists (24 per cent) or Presbyterians (23 per cent). Only half as many were Methodists (12 per cent), with a smaller percentage of Lutherans (7 per cent), Evangelical and United Brethren (8 per cent), Disciples (4 per cent), and Episcopalians (2 per cent) who prayed.

Further consideration of this interview in the light of the larger study shows that Mr. Sheraton did what the largest number (36 per cent) of the pastors would do: he helped the student to understand his decision. Since Joe was already in college, the pastor may not have felt it necessary to urge him to get academic training, which was a very common response of Disciples of Christ (38 per cent) and Baptist (41 per cent) pastors.

If Mr. Sheraton had told the student about his own call from God, one could safely assume that he was Baptist (21 per cent), Methodist (17 per cent), or Presbyterian (16 per cent). Less than 10 per cent of the pastors in other denominations studied mentioned to their young people their own personal commitments.

"The Honor of the Church"

Having read this analysis of one interview, a pastor may be intimidated by the exacting training required for a counseling ministry or be wearied by the amount

43

of time and concentration needed to deal with the personal concerns of each prospective minister or religious worker in his congregation. But the pastor gains true perspective as he lifts up his eyes and sees his sacred duty to individual souls under his care. Richard Baxter inspired pastors of his day by his own example and with such words as these:

We should know every person that belongeth to our charge; for how can we take heed to them if we do not know them? . . . All the flock being thus known, must afterwards be taken heed to. . . . Doth not a careful shepherd look after every individual sheep? And a good schoolmaster look after every individual scholar, both for instruction and correction? And a good physician look after every particular patient? And a good commander look after every individual soldier? Why then, should not the teachers, the pastors, the physicians, the guides of the Churches of Christ, take heed to every individual member of their charge? Christ himself, the great and good Shepherd, and Master of the Church, that hath the whole to look after, doth yet take care of every individual. He tells us that He is as the Shepherd that "leaveth the ninety and nine sheep in the wilderness, to seek after one that was lost"; or as the "woman that lighteth a candle and sweepeth the house and searcheth diligently to find the one groat that was lost; and having found it doth rejoice and call her friends and neighbors to rejoice"; and Christ telleth us that even in heaven there is joy over one sinner that repenteth.

The prophets are often sent to single men. Ezekiel is made a watchman over individuals and Paul warned every man, in all wisdom, that he might present every man perfect in Christ Jesus.[1]

The justification for time, energy, and training expended in personal counseling is summed up by Baxter in this sentence:

"The strength of Christians is the honor of the church." [2]

IV

A Theology for Church Vocations

One fact on which all Christians seem to agree is
that young men and women must be called into God's
service. The young people who are thus called need to
be able to interpret the voice which speaks to them.
To help in the interpretation of God's call is the responsibility of the religious counselor; too often the
counselor fails at this point. To help meet this need
in every pastor's ministry, this chapter contains four
central statements which are based upon passages in
the New Testament and their historical interpretation.

The Christian Calling

The Christian calling is God's call to men to accept
his salvation through Christ Jesus. In the letter to the
Ephesians Paul explains "calling" as the response of
man to God's plan for the good of man and for the
glory of God. Paul believed that all who accept God's
call are equal in his sight: Christ "has broken down
the dividing wall of hostility. . . . You are fellow citi-
zens with the saints and members of the household of
God" (Eph. 2:14–19).

Furthermore, all who accept God's call are challenged by Paul to lead a life worthy of their calling

(Eph. 4:1–5:2). In 1 Peter 2:9 Christians are proclaimed to be a "chosen race, a royal priesthood." Upon these and similar passages, such as Hebrews 9:11–28, congregational groups have derived a principle of individual competency under God in all matters of religion. Each believer is a priest, a minister to his brother.

The ministry as a calling is thus a responsibility upon every Christian. One of the earliest examples of this theme in American church life was Cotton Mather's pamphlet to laymen, *Essays To Do Good* (1710). Mather urged that everyone do good to his family and neighbors daily. Christ was to be served through every profession. The elders of the church should visit the congregation often to minister to both physical and spiritual needs. A "private meeting for religion," which ministers should attend only occasionally, was proposed for laymen. The laymen should minister to each other and discuss opportunities for "practical piety" in their community.

The social gospel movement continued this early emphasis upon following in the steps of the Master in all walks of life. In *The Christian Pastor and the Working Church* (1898) Washington Gladden urged pastors to enlist and direct the work of laymen so that laymen might take over the church organization, freeing the minister for pastoral duties. The success of Gladden's many-sided ministry testifies to the practicality of leadership training for laymen.

G. B. Willcox, of Chicago Theological Seminary,

gave even stronger expression to this idea. In *The Pastor Amidst His Flock* he stated that laymen can do many things which the pastor cannot. The rich man who backs up his proposals with money was one example. Young people influence their own sex and age in a way that adults cannot.

The "Louisville Plan" is a contemporary example of the Christian calling in action. Laymen from Protestant churches throughout Louisville meet every month with the officials and staffs of various institutions to study the needs and find ways of strengthening these agencies through community resources. Before the Mental Hygiene Society became fashionable, these dedicated laymen spearheaded a drive to appropriate adequate funds for mental hospitals and take the staff appointments out of partisan politics. Innumerable other examples are recorded in the literature distributed by Mr. George Stoll, the layman who founded this work.[1]

Varieties of Service

Within this Christian calling there are varieties of service, one of which is a church vocation. The essential experience, or "spiritual gift," is described in 1 Corinthians 12:1–11 as the working of the Holy Spirit in each believer to cause him to accept Jesus as Lord. Following this experience, many "gifts" are bestowed on all the members of the church for "varieties of service," in "varieties of working," and all for the "common good."

Paul further states that no one function shall have

more honor than any other in the body of Christ (1 Cor. 12:14–30). Martin Luther presented the same idea in his *Treatise on Good Works*. He protested against the Roman practice of considering daily work on a lower moral level than working in a convent, singing, playing the organ, saying the Mass, or going to Rome. He wrote, "All works, let their name be what it may, become great only when they flow from faith, the first, greatest, and noblest of works." [2]

According to Paul, the ministry has its primary authority in its functional service. The "gifts" to apostles, prophets, evangelists, pastors, and teachers are to be considered functional gifts "for the work of ministry, for building up the body of Christ" (Eph. 4:12). In the application of this principle, every believer is responsible for understanding the meaning of his calling. Religious leaders are not eliminated. Those who have gifts of religious leadership are given authority by the group to exercise their gifts for the benefit of all. Indeed, those who have the gifts of leadership are responsible for the stewardship of these gifts. They are duty bound to use their talents for the benefit of the church.

Two of the Church Fathers felt the results of this principle. Gregory Nazianzin was forcibly ordained by his father. Gregory, burning with resentment, fled to Pontus, but a year later he returned to take up his pastoral duties. John Chrysostom was dismayed to learn that he and a friend, Basil, were to be consecrated priests. At the last moment his courage failed him

49

and he fled, leaving Basil to be consecrated alone. Chrysostom later returned and became a priest and a leader in the church.

A modern example of a layman called to the ministry by other laymen was the ordaining of a famous Baptist pastor, George Truett. He was "simply appalled" by the action of the church, of which he was Sunday school superintendent, when they drafted him for the Christian ministry. But when every member of the church told him individually of their conviction that he should be a minister, he finally said, "I was thrown into the stream and had to swim."

There was no presumption that Nazianzin, Chrysostom, or Truett were not fulfilling the Christian calling before ordination. The reason for ordination was a recognition of their special personal qualities for full-time church leadership.

Evidence of Calling

Those who are called of God are to give evidence through their lives of their calling. John Wesley would often say to ordaining councils, "He thinks he has the grace; let us see if he has the gifts." Paul prayed for the Ephesians that every one of them would understand the meaning of his calling in relation to other people through the love of Christ (3:14–19). The Christian community may take the initiative in showing an individual how his gifts fit some particular function of the Christian calling (Acts 13:2–3).

In his pastoral epistles, Paul stressed the observation

of a man's living before he was set apart as a religious leader. Deacons were to be tested first; only when proved blameless should they serve (1 Tim. 3:10). Bishops were not to be new converts and were to be well thought of by outsiders. In their personal and domestic lives they were to be above reproach (1 Tim. 3:1–7).

When young people raise the question of their personal qualifications for a church vocation, pastors can suggest the following scriptural passages for meditation and self-examination: 1 Timothy 3:1–7; 2 Timothy 2:20–26; Titus 1:5–9; 2 Corinthians 4:1–6; 1 Peter 5:1–11. A later conversation as to the interpretation of these passages provides a fine opportunity for developing a lasting friendship with the young person, often what he most needs.

The Role of Other Christians

Those who enter a church vocation are called both by God and by fellow believers. They have a responsibility to God and to man for their vocational choice. The first example of this dual responsibility occurs in Acts 13:1–3. The Holy Spirit called Paul and Barnabas to the ministry, but they were called also through the church. The close connection between the work of the Christian community and the Holy Spirit is shown by the last phrase of verse 3 and the first phrase of verse 4: "They sent them off. So, being sent out by the Holy Spirit . . ."

Another example of this responsibility is found in 1 Timothy 3:1–7. Paul presented in these verses certain criteria by which the Christian community might discharge its responsibility to select worthy men who have been called to the office of bishop. Calvin based his requirements for the examinations of candidates in the Reformed Church upon this passage of Scripture. He stated that the call to the ministry consists of the secret call of God, which is indispensable but not known or regulated by the church, and the solemn call which belongs to the public order of the church and is subject to regulation.[3]

The challenge to serve as a servant appointed both by God and man rings in these words of Richard Baxter:

Men thought of a reformation to be given by God, but not of a reformation to be wrought on and by themselves. Little did they think of a reformation that must be wrought by their own diligence and unwearied labours, by earnest preaching and catechizing, and personal instructions, and taking heed to all the flock, whatever pains or reproaches it should cost them.[4]

When young men and women do not have an adequate understanding of the divine call of God and the personal requirements of his ministry among men, theologically trained men must interpret these things to them. Inadequate gifts and weak motivation do not empower a man to fill the pastoral office. A veteran Texas minister often warned students that "a hot sun and a slow mule has called many a man to preach."

It is a great privilege to interpret a church vocation

to those who give evidence of approval before God and men. Breath-taking adventures are before them. In his Yale lectures Dr. Raymond Calkins breathed this spirit when he said:

I cannot get away from the idea that, if a man is going to speak for God, God has got to choose him for the work. I am sorry for a good many people today. But on the whole the man I am the sorriest for is the man who stands before a Christian congregation without feeling that God has put him there.

There is no satisfaction like the satisfaction of a human being who stands before a company, large or small, and declares to them the oracle of God which it has been put in his mouth to speak. . . . The humblest preacher in the land if he be that kind of a preacher, can know a joy which no one else can know. And from my soul I envy the man who is going to taste it for the first time and know it for what it is. . . .[5]

V

Literature on Church Vocations

Literature can be a valuable aid in the pastor's guidance of those interested in a church vocation. In describing his call to the ministry John Bunyan stated that he searched not only the Scriptures but also Fox's *Arts and Monuments* before he made his decision. George Whitefield, pondering God's will for his life, was much impressed by William Law's *A Serious Call to a Devout and Holy Life*. The reading of the life of David Brainerd sent William Carey and Henry Martin to India and profoundly influenced such stalwart ministers as Payson, McCheyne, and Wesley. John Wesley's advice was that every preacher read carefully the life of David Brainerd.

Pastors will need at least two types of literature in their personal libraries: resource books, which they read for themselves, and books and pamphlets, which they lend or give to members of their congregations.

Resource Books

In addition to the biblical passages on the Christian calling, the pastor can study other books on the same subject, such as *The Glory of God in the Christian Calling* by Dr. W. O. Carver, *Christian Faith and My*

Job by Alexander Miller, or *God and the Day's Work* by Dr. Robert Calhoun. This last book is a popular presentation of his more weighty philosophical work, *God and the Common Life.*

Two studies of the ministry are now being published. The first is a series of three books under the editorship of H. Richard Niebuhr. *The Purpose of the Church and Its Ministry* and *The Ministry in Historical Perspective* are already available. The second study is by a sociologist, Samuel Blizzard. It is a job analysis of the ministry based on intensive interviews with ministers in the New York City area and questionnaires returned by ministers in some other parts of the United States. This valuable research will probably be available in 1957 or 1958.

A pastor needs an interpretation of the ministry in his own denomination, such as R. C. Walton's *The Gathered Community* or Robert Torbet's *The Baptist Ministry: Then and Now* for Baptists, and L. J. Trinterud's *The Forming of an American Tradition* for Presbyterians. Methodists will find a scholarly review of their ministry in the reports of Murray Leiffer (*The Methodist Ministry,* Report for 1948, 1952, etc.) and Ralph Felton (*New Ministers*). A Baptist study, *Theological Education in the Northern Baptist Convention,* was prepared in 1945 by Hugh Hartshorne and Milton Froyd.

Of more general help are such works as *Protestant Religious Vocations* by John Oliver Nelson, *An Enlistment Manual for Church Vocations* by John Oliver

Nelson, and *Counseling for Church Vocations* by Harold W. Ewing.

Materials for Distribution

Various types of literature, usually available from denominational offices, may be handed to young people who are interested in a church vocation.

Pastors and youth leaders can use discussion material. "How About My Career Choice?" or "Students Ask About Missions," available from the Joint Department of Christian Vocation, 297 Fourth Avenue, New York, will provoke lively comment. Much relevant material is contained in the *Recruitment Packet* distributed by the Methodist Publishing House. The Education Commission of the Southern Baptist Convention has published a series of pamphlets on vocations, including church vocations.

A number of promotional pamphlets are available. A series on foreign mission vocations, such as "If You Want to Be a Missionary Nurse," can be had from the Foreign Mission Board of the Southern Baptist Convention, Richmond 20, Virginia. "Keep That Dream Alive" is prepared for draftees by the Methodist Publishing House. "Out of Uniform into What?", "Women's Church Vocations," and "Possibly the Ministry" are available from the Joint Department of Christian Vocation, 297 Fourth Avenue, New York.

Several promotional booklets are attractively illustrated: "A Young Man's View of the Ministry" by S. M. Shoemaker, "Look at the Ministry" by J. O. Nelson, and "Look at the Missionary" by Winburn Thomas.

There is also a need for factual information. "We Have This Ministry" by J. O. Nelson gives a condensed report of many different types of church work. Qualifications and preparation for missionary service are discussed in "New Missionaries for New Days" by E. K. Higdon. *The Minister's Job* by Albert W. Palmer contains a chapter on "Self-Analysis for Ministers."

Even though a young person may have been a church member for years, he needs to know in detail the background of his own denomination. Representative books are listed at the end of this chapter.

The young person may also wish to know where his denomination, or section of it, fits into Reformation tradition. William Hordern's *A Layman's Guide to Protestant Theology* would help to meet this need. To understand his distinctive Reformation confession in contrast to the Roman Catholic Church, the young person should study *Primer for Protestants* by James Nichols, *The Things Most Surely Believed Among Us* by James A. Pike, or *Why I Am Not a Roman Catholic* by Kenneth N. Ross.

Devotional material is often helpful. The Bible contains passages on the Christian vocation (Matt. 6:33; 1 Cor. 12; Ephesians), church vocations (Rom. 10:15; Eph. 4; Mark 16:15; Matt. 13:46), and calls to life service (Ex. 3:1–15; Isa. 6). These and other passages should be studied in detail by the candidate.

Two series of books on the devotional life are now

available. The first, the World Devotional Classics series, contains such works as *The Journal of John Woolman* and *Christian Perfection* by John Wesley. The second, the Wycliffe Series of Christian Classics, contains inspiring autobiographies like *The Diary of David Brainerd.*

For private devotions, *A Diary of Private Prayer* by John Baillie and the *Southwell Litany* are particularly relevant to a church vocation.

The personal struggles of those called to a church vocation are revealed in autobiographies such as Augustine's *Confessions* and biographies like *The Story of John Frederick Oberlin* by A. F. Beard, *The Life of William Carey* by D. Pearce Carey, and contemporary stories such as *The Diary of a Dean* by Dean Inge, or *George W. Truett* by P. W. James.

Classics on the pastoral office should be studied. As the young person progresses in his personal sense of dedication, he will receive inspiration from those who have lived victoriously as pastors. Examples are Richard Baxter's *The Reformed Pastor,* Arthur Hewitt's *Highland Shepherds,* and John Oman's *Concerning the Ministry.* The work of a pastor as a counselor is described in *The Christian Pastor* by Wayne E. Oates.

Taking Stock of Pastoral Resources

Literature on church vocations, a relevant theology, and previous training in pastoral counseling are resources upon which ministers will draw continually in their dealings with young people. Chapters 2, 3, and 4 have outlined some of the more obvious materials which will be useful. However, several other problems remain. Pastors must not merely read about these resources; they must apply them in face-to-face relationships. Furthermore, their counsel will be most applicable if they know something of the typical problems which young people face in their preparation for life-work.

Therefore, the following chapters will seek to apply what has just been written to specific problems. The first and most formidable of these is the interpretation of a divine sense of mission.

Books on Various Denominations

The wise counselor will want to provide each counselee with some specific guidance in understanding his own denomination. One way to do this is to suggest or even to lend an appropriate book. Two or more suitable titles are given below for each of several major denominational families.

BAPTIST

BARNES, W. W. *The Southern Baptist Convention, 1845– 1953*. Nashville: Broadman Press, 1954.

DILLARD, JAMES E. *We Southern Baptists*. Nashville: Broadman Press, 1948.

JOHNSON, RALPH M., AND GOODWIN, R. DEAN. *Faith and Fellowship of American Baptists*. Philadelphia: Judson Press, 1951.

MEAD, FRANK S. *The Baptists*. Nashville: Broadman Press, 1954.

TORBET, ROBERT. *A History of the Baptists*. Philadelphia: Judson Press, 1950.

DISCIPLES OF CHRIST

GARRISON, WINFRED. *An American Religious Movement*. St. Louis: Christian Board of Publication, 1954.

SHORT, HOWARD E. *Doctrine and Thought of the Disciples of Christ*. St. Louis: Christian Board of Publication, 1951.

EPISCOPAL

HODGES, GEORGE. *The Episcopal Church*. New York: Morehouse-Gorham, 1938.

PIKE, JAMES A., AND PITTENGER, W. NORMAN. *The Faith of the Church*. Greenwich, Connecticut: Seabury Press, 1951.

METHODIST

CHERRY, CLINTON. *The Beliefs of a Methodist Christian*. Nashville: Tidings Press, 1949.

KERN, PAUL B. *Methodism Has a Message*. Nashville: Abingdon Press, 1941.

PRESBYTERIAN

HANZSCHE, WILLIAM THOMPSON. *Know Your Church!* Philadelphia: Westminster Press, 1946.

SMART, JAMES. *What a Man Can Believe*. Philadelphia: Westminster Press, 1943.

VI

Interpreting the Call

The concept of a call from God has been central to the biblical and historical motivation for a church vocation. How is this to be interpreted to modern young men and women who are concerned about a church vocation? Some ministers feel that any indecisiveness about a call on the part of a young person should be dealt with by immediate answers from the pastor. Others feel that in the beginning stages a young person needs a sympathetic listener more than he needs "correct" solutions from the pastor.

In *Pastoral Psychology*, November, 1955, the issue of "sudden conversion versus counseling" was raised concerning the following conversation between Pastor Hay and a high school student, Jim:

JIM: How did *you* know when you had the call of Christ?
HAY: It may be hard to explain fully, Jim. There wasn't any sudden flash or direct call. It was more of a growing realization of a need both within myself and in society. I saw a need for Christian witness and I had a slowly growing gnawing until I would try to do something about it. Is that what you had in mind, Jim?
JIM: Yeah, I think so. My sister, she's a Baptist, she asked me how I knew that Christ was calling me. I couldn't quite explain it to her. Well *(he trails off)*.

HAY: Well, let's see, Jim. Maybe together we can work on it. Would you say it was a quick flash or a slow growth?

JIM: It was a slow growth—and yet I'm not sure.

HAY: In other words, you have a two-way feeling as to whether Christ should call in a moment, or over a period of time. Kind of split inside yourself and can't quite explain the feeling deep inside you?

JIM: Yeah, that's it all right. I feel it down here, but I can't quite explain it. (*Here Jim became silent, and was plainly wrestling with himself. This lasted for about five minutes. Then Jim plainly relaxed, but still said nothing.*)

HAY: You're working too hard, Jim.

JIM: (*With a laugh*) You said it.

. . . .

HAY: How did you come to decide on this church vocation business, Jim?

JIM: Four years ago in the Blank Camp, I decided I'd like to do something for God. I thought about it for a while. Then last summer I felt it again, and it has stayed with me. I really want to be a preacher. Something happened.

HAY: You might say you had a religious experience?

JIM: Yeah. It's hard to explain (*here Jim gestures several times toward his abdomen, struggles for words, and then finally stops struggling*).

HAY: Something welling up from the inside?

JIM: That's it. It's just hard to explain. (*There followed another silence of several minutes, with Jim struggling.*)[1]

A minister wrote that this interview was unsatisfactory, since Jim's problem was not *inside* Jim. Rather, it was an issue which should be interpreted by Pastor Hay.

The Reverend Myron C. Madden replied to the minister's question by saying in part:

I do not believe that Pastor Hay or any other counselor can avoid the paradoxes of existence; nor can he shield the teen-ager from them. It is doubtful whether he should try. It is at this point that young people need personal support in the shape of thoughtful pastoral care. Care which, in fact, will serve as their supply line while they go out and do battle with the paradoxes.

Yes, the paradox is there. It is a stone of stumbling. The pastor ought to be a ready source of strength, not to help reduce the paradox, but to give Jim enough fortitude not to let it go until it yields its blessing. There is always the possibility that Jim could take one side of the paradox and deny the other so as to escape tension. Pastor Hay made no attempt to pressure him in either direction. He waited with a "friendly silence."

I felt that the pastor was wise in not intruding into the more private part of the struggle. Obviously Jim had a lot of feelings that were not yet ripe for verbalizing. This is often the paradox from the inside—expressed viscerally.

I cannot quite accept the fact that there are a group of "conversionist" ministers as opposed to a group of "counseling" ministers. No good counselor would rule out either the "quick flash" or the "slow growth." He would be willing to accept and discuss the facts either way.

The paradoxes are best born (and in some sense perhaps, resolved) in a fellowship. The pastor is the one who does most to manipulate the flow of the fellowship toward arid areas. He is a communications specialist, communicating himself and the fellowship to anyone in particular need standing under the bruising lashes of paradox.

My experience with teen-agers has taught me that they have inestimable resources to deal with paradox. They sometimes may need a spiritual pump-priming from pastor and church, but they do not want this to be a substitute for personal production.[2]

The question of when the minister should talk about the call of God has been placed early in this chapter for a particular reason. Pastors need to know *when* to speak as well as *what* to speak.

To meet both these needs, this chapter contains biblical and historical examples of a call from God, plus a discussion of modern attempts to interpret the call experience and some suggestions for the use of this material in counseling.

Biblical Examples of the Call

Many pastors might assert the need to explain the call from God to a young person struggling to make a decision. Strangely enough, only a fraction of them actually used the Bible in such an explanation. Only forty-five of the fifteen hundred seminary students studied said that their pastor read any Scripture on God's call when they conversed about a church vocation.

Yet there is a wealth of biblical material. It may be arranged into such categories as the general call of God to all men, the special call to a church vocation, and examples of God's personal call to men.

Examples of the general call of God to all men are found in Ephesians 4:1–3, 2 Timothy 1:9, and Romans 10:14. All men who accept God's call are challenged by Paul to lead a life worthy of their calling:

I therefore, a prisoner for the Lord, beg you to lead a life worthy of the calling to which you have been called, with all lowliness and meekness, with patience, forbearing one another in love, eager to maintain the unity of the Spirit in the bond of peace (Eph. 4:1–3).

Each man or woman who accepts God's call has a responsibility to live as priest or minister: "But you are a chosen race, a royal priesthood, a holy nation, God's own people, that you may declare the wonderful deeds of him who called you out of darkness into his marvelous light" (1 Pet. 2:9).

"To him who loves us and has freed us from our sins by his blood and made us a kingdom, priests to his God and Father, to him be glory and dominion for ever and ever. Amen" (Rev. 1:5–6).

Just as there is one general call to all men to accept Christ's salvation, so there is one Spirit that moves in men despite their varied occupations. The scriptural truth that God calls men to many types of work has been emphasized by such writers as Dr. Robert Calhoun (*God and the Common Life*), Emil Brunner (*The Divine Imperative*), Alexander Miller (*Christian Faith and My Job*) and W. R. Forrester (*Christian Vocation*). Paul summarized this truth in 1 Corinthians 12:4–11:

Now there are varieties of gifts, but the same Spirit; and there are varieties of service, but the same Lord; and there are varieties of working, but it is the same God who inspires them all in every one. To each is given the manifestation of the Spirit for the common good. To one is given through

the Spirit the utterance of wisdom, and to another the utterance of knowledge according to the same Spirit, to another faith by the same Spirit, to another gifts of healing by
the one Spirit, to another the working of miracles, to another prophecy, . . . to another various kinds of tongues,
to another the interpretation of tongues. All these are inspired by one and the same Spirit, who apportions to each
one individually as he wills.

A second biblical use of "call" comes from Jesus and
Paul. Both of them spoke directly concerning a specific
sense of Christian vocation to which one is called. Jesus
lamented the few laborers for a great harvest (Matt.
9:38), challenged his disciples to see the ripe harvest
(John 4:35), gave them specific instructions in early
missionary activity (Matt. 10), assured them that they
were kept by his own choice (John 15:16), and sent
them forth into the whole world with the gospel
(Matt. 28:19–20; Acts 1).

Paul presented the necessity for preachers to be
called of God if men are to hear and believe (Rom.
10:14–17). He wrote of prophets and teachers who la-
bor for the common good (1 Cor. 12:7, 27–28), and of
evangelists and pastors gifted by God (Eph. 4:12) "for
the equipment of the saints, for the work of ministry,
for building up the body of Christ." He gave specific
instructions to Timothy for the qualifications of pastors
(1 Tim. 3:1–7) and for the conduct of young pastors
in their new office (1 and 2 Tim.).

The apostle Peter gave a strong ethical emphasis in
his advice to pastors (1 Pet. 5:1–5).

Third, there are examples of God's personal call to chosen men. The most detailed of these is the call of Isaiah "in the year that King Uzziah died" (Isa. 6:1–8). Other Old Testament examples of God's call to individuals are the calls of Abraham (Gen. 12:1–4), Moses (Ex. 3:1–15), Samuel (1 Sam. 3:1–21), David (2 Sam. 16:1–13), and Jeremiah (Jer. 1:4–10, 17–19).

In the New Testament, Jesus called his disciples from the seashore (Mark 1:16–20), from public office (Luke 5:27–32), and from another teacher (John 1:29–42). The disciples recruited others (John 1:40–51). The last of the apostles was called by the risen Lord (Acts 9:1–9) and restored to health by the faith of a disciple (Acts 9:13–19).

Historical Examples

Very few pastors, ranging from 3 per cent of the Lutherans to 21 per cent of the Baptists, told young people about their personal call from God. Examples of God's call in the experience of great pastors are given here so that the pastor may illustrate the variety of ways in which God has dealt with his servants. These short sketches show differences, not only between periods of history and denominations but also, and most strikingly, between individuals because of temperament or family background.

Baptist.—Baptists have always given much emphasis to a divine call as a prerequisite for the pastoral office. This is still true today. In 1952, thirty-three of fifty-six students questioned in a class at the Southern Baptist Theological Seminary stated that God's call was their primary reason for entering the ministry. Forty-four per cent of Northern Baptist ministers gave a similar answer in 1945. Conversely, only 16 per cent of the students in an interdenominational study of 1933 felt a sense of divine compulsion or calling.[3]

One of the earliest Baptists, John Bunyan (1628–88), described his call in these words:

For after I had been about five or six years awakened, and helped myself to see both the want and worth of Jesus Christ our Lord, and also enabled to venture my soul upon him, some of the most able among the saints with us . . . did perceive that God had counted me worthy to understand something of his will in his holy and blessed work, and had given me utterance, in some measure, to express what I saw to others for edification. Therefore they desired me, and that with much earnestness, that I would be willing at some times to take in hand, in one of the meetings, to speak a word of exhortation unto them.

Which though at the first it did much dash and abash my spirit, yet being still by them desired and intreated, I consented to their request, and did twice . . . but in private, though with much weakness and infirmity, discover my gift amongst them. At which they not only seemed to be, but did solemnly protest, as in the sight of the great God, they were both affected and comforted; and gave thanks to the Father of mercies for the grace bestowed on me.

After this sometimes, when some of them did go into the country to teach, they would also that I should go with them; . . . privately still . . . I did sometimes speak a word of admonition unto them also; which they, as the other, received, with rejoicing at the mercy of God to me-ward, professing their souls were edified thereby.

Wherefore, to be brief, at last, being still desired by the church, after solemn prayer to the Lord, with fasting, I was more particularly called forth, and appointed to a more ordinary and public preaching of the word. . . ." [4]

Bunyan had been encouraged by certain Scriptures and Fox's *Acts and Monuments* before he made his decision. But he still felt guilty and began his preaching by "condemning all flesh." However, after two years he "felt sure peace and comfort through Christ" and altered his preaching accordingly.

Another famous Baptist preacher was called into the ministry by a congregation before he had openly accepted God's call to his own life. George W. Truett wrote: "Wednesday night of that week came, and to my utter amazement, the pastor, following the visiting preacher's sermon, turned abruptly to me and said, 'Brother George, won't you exhort these hesitating people to turn to Christ for his great salvation and service?'" He was carried away in his exhortation, walking up and down the aisle.

Then he felt he was a spectacle, and went home in deep humiliation. His mother kissed him and said, "My boy, all that is the temptation of Satan, to silence you as a witness for Christ." She added, "I doubt if ever in all your life you will give a more effective testimony for Christ than you gave tonight." "From that hour on, wherever I went, godly men and women would call me aside and searchingly say to me: 'Oughtn't you to give your life to the preaching of the glorious gospel of Christ?'" [5]

Truett did not become a minister then. Instead, he taught school for a while, then went to Hiawassee Academy as founder and principal. He was noted for personal evangelism and public speaking. When he moved from the academy to Texas, many people in the Sunday school of which he became superintendent told him that he should preach. He did not agree, because he considered himself unworthy of the ministry.

On a certain Saturday in 1890 the church voted to ordain him as a minister. Truett implored them to desist: "You have me appalled; you simply have me appalled!" He talked to his mother, who said, "Son, those are praying people. These are God's people. And you saw how they felt. They felt that they couldn't—even in the face of your plea, your protest, your exhortation to delay—they couldn't delay. It was a whole church in solemn conference assembled." He was ordained the next day.

Congregational.—A stirring and influential autobiography which appeals to young ministers and missionary candidates is *The Life and Diary of David Brainerd,* a Congregational Christian. This dedicated young man could have benefited from the right pastoral counsel but instead received the worst possible. After becoming very strict and watchful over his thoughts, words, and actions, he devoted himself to the ministry at the age of twenty. His melancholy disposition was reinforced by a minister with whom he lived, who advised him to associate only with grave people—old ones at that. In the midst of his struggles, while walking through a

70

grove trying to pray, "unspeakable glory" seemed to open his soul.

With renewed conviction Brainerd entered Yale. But his formal education was cut short when he was expelled from Yale for speaking privately to a friend about the pathetic praying of a tutor. He continued his preparation for the ministry in the home of a pastor and was ordained a missionary to the Indians. His depressions—and consumption—continued, but he was strengthened by the prayers and attention of friends. Finally his physical weakness prevented the continuation of his desired but hazardous labors. He died at twenty-nine.

A less melancholy and more tranquil decision for the ministry was recorded by Washington Gladden in his *Recollections*. Gladden recalled a happy childhood. When he left home, he drifted away from "strict sabbath-attendance" but was recalled by an evangelistic meeting. He felt after this experience that the kingdom of God must be realized in the world. To do his part, he went to Williams College and then taught school. He read much theology with a young minister who lived in the same boardinghouse. When Gladden preached a sermon for this young man, his friend urged him to be licensed as a Congregational minister to preach in schoolhouses. This was the prompting which led Gladden definitely into the ministry.[6]

Episcopal.—The experience of Washington Gladden is a transition from the definite calls of men like Bunyan and Brainerd to the absence of any such concept in the decision of Phillips Brooks for the Episcopal ministry. Phillips Brooks (1835–93) came from three generations of Puritan pastors. At the age of six he was impressed by the strong personality of a new minister, Dr. A. H. Vinton. Later, when Brooks failed as a teacher at Boston Latin School, he was encouraged to study for the ministry.

For some months young Brooks brooded over what to do. Then he called on Dr. Vinton and asked about steps in preparation for the ministry. Dr. Vinton said confirmation was customarily required before one became a candidate, and that confirmation was usually preceded by conversion. Although Phillips said he did not know what conversion meant, Dr. Vinton recommended that he study at Alexandria Seminary. Beyond his father and mother, Brooks took no one else into his counsels. He wrote to friends, "Consider me here at the seminary without debating how I got here." [7]

A more public decision is recorded by another Episcopalian, George Whitefield (1714–70). While a student at Oxford University he had a dream that he would see God on Mount Sinai. "A gentlewoman to whom I told it said, 'George, this is a call from God,'" but when he told his mother she said, "Hold thy tongue!" [8]

Whitefield joined Wesley's "holy club." He was much impressed by Law's *Serious Call to a Devout and Holy Life*. Friends urged his immediate ordination, but he was not yet twenty-one, and diocesan rule was twenty-three. His bishop asked to see him and said that he would ordain Whitefield any time he wished it. Whitefield needed help to remove the hindrance, "not a novice," from his own mind. He besought his friends not to push him into the ministry yet. As they continued to urge him, he began to think he was fighting against God's will. So, strictly examining himself by Paul's qualifications to Timothy, he decided to ask for ordination. He tried to compose some sermons, but blocked. He consulted several clergymen; one said he was an enthusiast. Another said the call might come in that way and promised to pray for him. The Bishop was gracious and encouraging.

At his ordination, Whitefield said that he felt like Samuel as a little child standing before the Lord. "When the Bishop laid his hands upon my head, my heart was melted down, and I offered up my whole spirit, soul, and body, to the service of God's sanctuary." He returned to Oxford, obtained his degree, and became one of the truly great preachers of his generation.

Methodist.—An example of a Methodist's call to the ministry is given by Edwin Hughes, who stated simply in his autobiography, "I was made a minister." Explaining this, he said:

The title of this volume, *I Was Made a Minister,* is taken from Paul. . . . All my life bore in that ministerial direction. I had the experiences of a parsonage in childhood so that I might bear them forward into other years. Forced changes from one college to another meant that I was being carried onward to a clerical career. This was not all of my own choosing. There were a few years in which the thought of the ministry was almost a torture. Yet the actual decades have given me a commentary on the way in which hate can change to love. While I do not sympathize with the overdone counsel, "Do not enter the ministry if you can help it," I still declare that I have had no religious experience more definite than my call to preach. . . . Though not irrestible, my ministerial life has never ceased to be a "calling." [9]

A more tempestuous decision led Sam Jones into the ministry. Jones felt a conviction to preach soon after the death of his father, who asked that they meet in heaven, and his conversion under the preaching of his grandfather the following Sunday. He sought the advice of several pastors. One said, "You are called to preach; you can come willingly into it, or you can be whipped into it, or you will lose your religion if you refuse." The last point caused him to make the definite decision for evangelism.[10]

Fifteen more examples of the sense of divine mission among Methodists may be found in *My Call to Preach*, compiled by E. A. Hunter.

Presbyterian.—The life of a famous 19th century Presbyterian, Henry Ward Beecher (1813–87), shows the blighting effects of a loveless minister-father. Henry Ward hated the noisy house in which he lived with four older brothers and sisters, his father's hypocrisy and dull sermons, and his stepmother's coldness. "A hermit could not have been more solitary," he said.[11] In desperation he sought the help of a renowned "saver of souls," Asahel Nettleton, who said, "Go away, boy!" Returning home, he found his stepmother praying for her own soul.

The father assumed that all his boys, like himself, would be ministers. Therefore, Henry was sent to the Boston Latin School, the Mount Pleasant Classical School, Amherst College, and to Lane Seminary when his father became president. Admiring and yet abhorring his father, Henry did what was expected of him. He reaped the reward of this type of compromise in Plymouth Church, Brooklyn. "His hunger for publicity, for the limelight, for the outward trappings of power, led Henry Ward Beecher into countless minor absurdities in these closing years of his life. He never seemed to grow up." [12]

Friendlier influences led another Presbyterian, Henry Drummond, toward the ministry. While a student at Edinburg, he was so impressed by a mission service that he told his father that he wished to enter the ministry. At this time he shared lodgings with divinity students who gave him friendly counsel. Then nineteen years old, he felt most grateful for the counsel of ministers and evangelists he met in Edinburg. One of these was Dwight Moody, for whom Drummond began to lead young men's meetings. In 1884 he began his own work with students. [13]

Summary.—Most of the varieties of a call experience have appeared in these brief biographies. The long struggle of Brainerd appears along with the sudden decision of Jones. The timid hesitancy of Bunyan contrasts with the lifetime confidence of Hughes. The debilitating effects of Henry Ward Beecher's growth under a minister-father were turned to a better advantage by Hughes. Opposed to the importance of a definite call in men like Bunyan is the almost complete indifference of young Brooks. Brooks satisfied his friends by letters of his decision. Whitefield sought the counsel of friends. Drummond profited by ministerial counsel; Brainerd suffered because of it.

After such a survey, one may say with the apostle Paul, "There are varieties of working, but it is the same God who inspires them all in every one" (1 Cor. 12:6) .

A Typical Call Experience

The historical examples just presented show the great variety of ways in which men come to know God's will for their lives.

A comprehensive study of the call experience has been made by Dr. Winston Crawley, Secretary for the Orient, Foreign Mission Board, Southern Baptist Convention. By questionnaire he studied the call of sixteen hundred Baptist missionaries and mission volunteers. The picture of the "normal call experience" which he presents might be typical or average in some other denominations, probably Methodist or Presbyterian.

The average mission volunteer came from a small town and from a middle class home. His parents were Baptists, having a definitely Christian home atmosphere, active in their church, and interested in missions. He was in the upper third of his public school class in academic work, and probably also in athletic and cultural activities and in special abilities, such as music and public speaking. He was one of the minority who did not join the common worldly practices of those around him. All in all, that average volunteer was well above the general level of youth—socially, mentally, culturally, and morally.

Further, the average mission volunteer became a Christian early in life, by a relatively calm conversion experience. He was an unusually active church member, showing more than ordinary interest in church organizations and activities, in religious conventions and summer encampments. He attended a Baptist College. His reading included religious books. He had personal devotional habits including daily Bible reading and prayer. He was interested in missions and comparatively well informed on the subject. Furthermore, he was concerned about his personal witness to non-Christians.

To continue further the description of the imagined "average" Southern Baptist missionary: In his late teens he first felt a call to foreign missions (preceded, in the case of the male volunteer, by a call to the ministry some years earlier). The call came to him gradually, rather than in a sudden dramatic experience. It was a call to do educational and evangelistic work, and in a particular country. After brief hesitation to make certain of its validity, he accepted his call willingly. There was no uniform determining influence in the feeling of the missionary call—rather a combination of influences, with some person (probably a missionary) outstanding. The evidences of call were chiefly subjective and spiritual, prominent among them being an abiding conviction of personal call. His missionary aim, the average volunteer felt, was to make Christ known (with all that such knowledge involved) to people of other lands and races.

A further observation from the data obtained was that the characteristics of the call experience changed with the passage of time. There was evidence in later years of interest in more different types of work, of a younger age at the feeling of call and at commitment to it, and of a growing percentage of volunteers from the city. The ratio of volunteers to church membership was declining in some of the older Southeastern states and advancing in those nearer the Southwestern "frontier." The definitely Christian home atmosphere seemed less prominent. Church religious training, however, was becoming more intensive. To an increasing proportion of volunteers the call was coming gradually, but the number accepting without struggle was declining. There was indication also of greater variety of aim.[14]

Contemporary Interpretations

The Crawley study represents one current interpretation of the "call." It contains a comprehensive review of biographical and historical works which illustrate the call to foreign missions. However, only the general characteristics of mission volunteers are described, such as length of schooling, amount of Bible reading and prayer at home, and time of conversion and call. Statements by missionaries concerning their motivation for mission service are presented without analysis by Dr. Crawley. There is no discussion of the difficulties of assuming that a person's written statement represents his innermost conviction or of the problem of evaluating what a person gives as his reason for mission service against how he lives as a mission student.

By simply recording evidence without critical examination, Dr. Crawley has at least presented original statistical and personal material without distortion. On the other hand, two earlier studies went too far in the opposite direction. They attempted to demonstrate the conditioning factors leading to a church vocation without any consideration of conscious motivation.

The presuppositions of one of these men, Philip Alaimo, excluded "the factors functioning in the individual's present life, his present ideas and ideals, his desires and aspirations, his thinking and theological positions, his general outlook at present and his hope for the future." [15] A more desiccated and wooden study of human beings can hardly be imagined! The other author, Abbott Herman, confined his study to "natural, social processes," and did not look for supernatural processes.

The deterministic presuppositions of Dr. Herman prevented him from recognizing the dynamic interactions of real persons. For example, he presented short excerpts from single interviews with five nontheological students to prove that "chance factors" caused them to give up previous ideas of entering the ministry. Actually, the "chance factors" were severe clashes with representatives of the ministry, such as a pastor, which naturally discouraged the young man from pursuing that vocation. From these five instances Dr. Herman generalized that "chance factors" are determinative and ignored the cases of men who continued into the ministry by dismissing their motivation as "an allegedly mystical experience." He asserted his search for "the utmost objectivity," yet he stated without any supporting evidence that the "call" to the ministry results from vivid suggestions by religious persons who like to tell "such stories." [16]

The failure of these two studies does not mean that personal interviews with students cannot yield dependable data. But it does mean that the data and its interpretation must be conducted within the limits imposed by certain accepted methods of research.

An example of a more reasonable interpretation of data on the personality and cultural factors that appear in divinity students is the study of Yale Divinity School students by Robert Smith in 1948. A conclusion of that study points up the pastor's importance in young people's decisions for a church vocation: "The most frequent factor mentioned by the men as influencing their specific vocational choice within the total field of religious work was the association with representatives and programs of the specific areas of religious work." [17]

Because the question of religious motivation is so complex, psychologists are now concentrating upon one aspect of this problem: psychological qualifications for a church vocation. Some psychologists are keeping records for future research on their routine testing of candidates for admission to theological schools. Others have worked with professors of pastoral care to prepare reports on their psychological testing and make recommendations to denominational offices. Several student psychologists are doing research in this area, although it is uncertain as to how much theological preparation they have had for such work. In April,

1955, interested pastors, theological professors, and psychologists met with Elmer Million, Department of the Ministry, National Council of Churches, for some preliminary conversations about psychological testing for theological students. Conclusions of this conference may be obtained from his office, 257 Fourth Avenue, New York 10, New York. A table is included which displays the great variety of psychological tests now being given in a majority of theological schools in the United States.

The Educational Testing Service, Princeton, N. J., began in 1956 a three-year study of the ministry under the direction of Dr. Samuel Cobb. Ministers, theological professors, and denominational representatives of many Protestant groups are represented on the board of directors for this project. The problem is complex; definitive conclusions will not be available for several years.

The Pastor's Use of This Material

These "raw materials" from the Bible, biographies of great pastors, and contemporary research will be valuable only if the pastor molds them to meet the individual needs of those who consult him about a church vocation. It is difficult to describe with any accuracy how the call of God is to be explained by a pastor or just how it will be revealed to a particular young person. The variety of call experiences in the Scriptures and in the lives of representative ministers challenges every counselor to lay aside his own preconceptions and reverently seek to know how God is making his will known in a young life. Even though the pastor, like Eli of old, may say to himself, "It is the Lord," his counsel must encourage the young seeker to know for himself, to say from his own heart, "Speak, Lord, for thy servant heareth."

Unless the pastor remembers this scriptural truth he may do all the speaking and give little opportunity for the young person to tell how the Spirit of God is dealing with him, and the interview will become merely another sermon by the pastor. One seminary student revealed his frustration by saying:

The minute I told my pastor that I was thinking about the ministry he said, "You just wait a year, and if God still calls you, you know it's real." He didn't ask me any questions or ask if I already knew God was calling me. Instead, he gave a half-hour history of how he was the only one of four classmates who finished college and entered the ministry. He told how he persevered under trying circumstances while his buddies ended up with menial jobs. He then dismissed me without a prayer. I had no chance to get in a word. I wanted so much to tell him of my call and the surrender I had made to God, but he gave me no opportunity to relate any of my happiness. . . .

If I become the right kind of pastor, I hope that I can help the individual who comes to me to relate his experience fully while I listen attentively and only ask an occasional question. Then with the person's permission we would read appropriate Scriptures and have prayer. I would expect us to have several sessions together. I would pray for the revelation of God to both of us. My own advice would come last.

To assist one with only a dawning awareness of a divine compulsion, the pastor will first want to know just how far along the individual is in his own thinking about a call. The pastor may ask for the person's opinion about a sense of mission, about his compulsion to enter a church vocation, or about his basic motivation for this work. If the person makes light of these things, the pastor can point out times of discouragement when a man must have a deep sense of commitment to continue in the ministry. He can illustrate the way a sense of conviction in preaching has moved the hearts of men even though the spoken words were simple. From personal experience the pastor can dramatize the confidence which laymen place in a minister who combines faith and a sense of the eternal with administrative know-how and common sense.

If the person is happy to give some description of his sense of mission, the pastor may wish to show him how his feelings are confirmed by the call of men in the Bible or in history. He may reassure the person that many of his problems are common to all those making this decision, or that he may have confidence in the fact that his background is similar to that of many others already in a church vocation. Through such counsel young people are encouraged to identify themselves with the highest and best in the Christian faith and to use great pastors or biblical personalities as patterns for their own growth.

Most seminary students report taking from one to three years to make their decisions for a church vocation. Most of the decisions (53 per cent) were made after much inner struggle. Such information as has been presented in this chapter will give young people something definite to think about during the time of decision. As the pastor communicates this information and suggests some of the reading material mentioned in chapter 5, he is cultivating interest in the right direction and stimulating steady growth toward a church vocation. A parent may plant the seed, the pastor may cultivate it, but God gives the growth (1 Cor. 3:6).

VII

Creative Problems of Vocational Growth

The biographies and autobiographies of great pastors reveal the intense personal struggles through which they grew in grace toward the high calling of the ministry. These men found problems at every stage in their pastoral maturing. Today young men and women grapple with similar personal concerns. They meet these crises over a period of years as they develop toward a church vocation.

Inquiries answered by ministerial students show that young men and women have certain types of problems at varying times in their development toward a church vocation. For convenience these problems are here divided into three groups: problems at the time of decision for a church vocation, problems in college, and problems in the seminary or divinity school.

Many young people handle their own difficulties. The students who answered the 1954 questionnaire showed a healthy sense of independence. They did not wish to be coddled or made dependent. Sometimes they were forced into independent judgments because there was no pastoral counselor to whom they felt free to talk. One student in this position wrote:

During the time preceding my call and at the time of my surrender I was without the counsel of anyone. The problem was just between the Lord and myself. I had no one to whom I could confidently turn where I was, and therefore the problem was settled on my knees before the Lord in prayer. . . . I, like many others, had been neglected too often and had to make my own decisions without adequate counsel from my father. So, when the time came for me to make a decision, I made it in the light of what I knew by myself. It was hard this way, but there is no doubt about the reality of my call.

Others sought help with difficult and puzzling problems of readjustment to a church vocation, but found none.

Those young people who did find a few moments with their pastors often did not receive the information they sought. Pastors have seldom thought of vocational growth as a process which covers a period of years. Consequently, they have not anticipated this development in advice based on the inherited experience of the Christian community. They have not been attentive to the problems involving the whole personality of candidates for church vocations or dealt with them therapeutically through group discussions or a series of private interviews.

These are strong statements. They are conclusions drawn from the statistics and comments of the 1954 study. Less than 10 per cent of the fifteen hundred students in seven denominations had a formal interview with their pastor, although a majority of them talked to him informally. Over half of the students had never attended a group conference on church vocations, and only a third of those who attended felt that the conference was helpful. The highest percentage of formal interviews (12 per cent) was among Episcopalians. The lowest was among Disciples (4 per cent) and Methodists (3 per cent). Disciples led in the percentage of informal conversations on several occasions (74 per cent). One significant result of the high percentage of Episcopal formal interviews was the large number (50 per cent) of Episcopal students who checked: "As a result of your conversation, you felt better able to evaluate your decision." The next highest number who checked this point were Disciples (39 per cent).

Disciples received almost twice as much help with their problems through group conferences (26 per cent) as the other six denominations (15 per cent). The Disciples' group conferences were regional (13 per cent) or state (10 per cent) or in their own churches (6 per cent). It is also interesting that more Disciples (31 per cent) than any other communion (average 16 per cent) were helped by personal conferences with a professional church worker before they had definitely made up their minds for a church vocation. Was the regional conference the time when they could see a religious leader privately?

The counseling of these young persons is a responsibility that moves from local pastor to professor of Bible to seminary professor as the student moves from the church to the college and finally to the seminary.

There is hardly a church, college, seminary, or denomination that has developed a system—or even a concept—of personal ministry to the candidate through his total vocational development.

Concerns of Youth in Decisions

The problems of youth surround the decision for a church vocation. Sixty-three per cent of the decisions were made between the ages of sixteen and twenty-two. Counselors had sufficient time to work with these young people, for a period of from one to three years elapsed between the occasion when they first thought of this work and their definite public decisions.

The surrender to this sacred calling did *not* follow failures in other types of work. A majority of the students were in high school or college when they made their decisions. Among those who were working, as has been noted, a much higher percentage than the national average were engaged in professional or clerical work before they entered a church vocation. The unrealistic advice to "not enter the ministry if you can do anything else" was voiced by only 5 per cent of the ministers consulted by students.

The three major problems mentioned in the 1954 study were: financing an education, feelings of personal unworthiness, and ambitions to enter another vocation.

Although these were the major concerns of men in all seven denominations, those students who entered the ministry at an older age were especially concerned about having ambitions to enter another vocation, giving up an income, and supporting a family. Missouri Synod Lutheran students, who made their decisions early, had few of these concerns. Instead, leaving home was two and one-half times as large a problem to them as it was in all other denominations.

Baptists, Methodists, and Evangelical United Brethren were the groups most concerned about insufficient educational preparation. Disciples and Lutherans were the least worried about giving up personal habits unbecoming to a church vocation.

In all denominations, students commented on the great need for spiritual and financial support from church workers and the Christian community. For example, think how attentive listening and judicious support would have helped this student:

Not known by anyone who is an influential Presbyterian. Very few of my own people attend the Presbyterian church. I was reared in the country on a farm. Poor family economically, country school, no background in culture. Very little encouragement, a sense of futility in face of overwhelming odds.

It is very difficult to lay out the "secrets" of counseling young people with such problems. Each pastor, religious educator, and denominational worker has a particular personality of his own, and he will face an individual who needs help in his own way and for his own needs. Perhaps the most general suggestion is that the pastoral counselor seek to create a warm, consistent, and lasting relationship in which the young person will find security and a sense of belonging to a noble calling. When the counselor is too busy for a personal interview (often more of an excuse than a fact), he should try to introduce young people to others who are interested in a similar vocation. As one student said:

The most helpful thing to me in the period following my decision was the close friendship with several interested in the same calling and working with them. They provided help by giving me a sense of security during periods of emotional conflict.

If the pastor will take more than a few minutes with each young seeker after God's will, he will soon discover the deeper significance of the student questionnaire phrase: "Feelings of personal unworthiness." Some students are conscious of real inadequacies, such as the obstacles faced by the Presbyterian quoted three paragraphs above. The pastor can be encouraging if he says, "You have some real problems to overcome, but the continuation of your college education will provide you with opportunities to be with people who know something about culture. Speech departments in college and seminary can help you with your accent and grammar. Our church will help you financially so that you'll have a little time to listen to outstanding speakers, attend concerts, and take a date to dinner."

This type of response shows that the pastor knows what the student faces and can suggest resources for personality development. Such an approach also avoids the Pollyanna phrases: "I'm sure that everything will work out." "It's not really as bad as it seems." "You can do it if you really want to." These statements suggest that the pastor is callous, anxious, or/and pushing away the seeker so that he can hurry off to some meeting.

Even less effective is the use of religion as magic. Counselors promote this concept by saying, "Just pray and it will all work out," or "Have faith, that's all." These words may be easily interpreted by the young person to mean that he can move blandly ahead without serious consideration of the future, since realistic obstacles will dissolve if he prays hard enough. A brief recall of the life of Jesus shows the thoughtlessness of such pastoral advice. Jesus prayed in the Garden as no man ever prayed before. He was crucified the next day. Obviously, therefore, faith and prayer do not make any Christian the exception to the struggles of mankind. Our Lord in human form "humbled himself and became obedient unto death, even death on a cross" (Phil. 2:8).

Only half the truth is told in the advice, "Just have faith and pray." The whole truth is: have faith that God will work with his children through all trials. This is the truth expressed by the apostle Paul: "We know that in everything God works for good with those who love him, who are called according to his purpose" (Rom. 8:28). Romans 5:1–5 and 1 Peter 5:1–11 give eternal courage because the disciples had measured their opposition and found it far short of the breadth

and length and height and depth of the love of Christ
(Eph. 3:14–19). The mature prayer is that God will
give strength to the believer through success and failure, through tribulation and prosperity.[1]

Young men and women who know their unworthiness and handicaps can be helped by the pastor who
confesses with them that God's thoughts are not our
thoughts yet knows that God in Christ has chosen the
foolish and weak in the eyes of the world to shame the
wise and strong (1 Cor. 1:18–31).

But what if the young person mentions *no* feelings
of unworthiness? Or, more difficult to detect, suppose
that he speaks superficially of a few sins and reveals a
hard core of legalistic righteousness? Certainly the pastor is no infallible judge who may shake a finger in
this "Pharisee's" face. But perhaps out of careful listening the minister may hold the self-mirror so surely
that the youth can see himself as God sees him, or
others see him, or he inwardly sees himself.

Dr. Mann, a professor of religion, found this type of
thinking in the mind of Allen, a college sophomore.
Allen came to see Dr. Mann about Coleen, his fiancée.

ALLEN: You see, Doctor, I want to marry a pure girl. But I
  have found that Coleen does not meet my standards.
DR. MANN: How is that?
ALLEN: Well, when we became engaged I asked her if she
  had ever kissed anyone but me. She said yes. I didn't
  like it, but I loved her, so I forgave her. That was last
  summer when I was home. Well, since she's been at
  A.C. [a near-by college] I only see her on week ends.

Last Saturday I asked her if she'd been out any during the week with any R.O.T.C. students, and she said yes. I told her the engagement was off. She cried and told me she'd never do it again. But I can't risk marrying her. My future would be ruined. (*Pause.*)

DR. MANN: Your future?

ALLEN: Yes. I'm thinking of becoming a minister. I wanted to pick out a pure woman who would uphold Christian standards. You can't be too careful as a minister, you know. You agree with me, don't you?

DR. MANN: Ah, you just left Coleen like that?

ALLEN: Certainly! She must learn her lesson. Oh, I'll take her back later, but she must be disciplined. She must understand that I want a perfect girl. I intend to write and tell her so.

DR. MANN: I would be very interested in meeting a perfect person.

ALLEN: Oh, well, we all sin. I do, sometimes. But you know how it is. I mean, you have to keep your code of honor even if it means hurting somebody else.

DR. MANN: Have you ever known any people like that?

ALLEN: Sure. I try to be as perfect as possible. The Bible commands it. I don't intend to say one thing in the pulpit and live another.

DR. MANN: I don't want you to do that either. That's why I've been asking these questions. Coleen doesn't meet *your* ideal of perfect. What would it be like if she pretended to meet it just to please you?

ALLEN: Well, that's why I intend to send this letter explaining it all to her. Do you think I should send it? Is this what a minister should do?

DR. MANN: I wonder if you'd be interested in talking with me some about your ideas of what a minister should be?

ALLEN: Sure, any time.

The interview concluded with this statement. It is difficult to say how effective it was. On the one hand, Dr. Mann listened enough to see the perfectionistic trends in Allen; he tried to bring the interview to a point so that Allen would begin to see the disparity between his self-idealization as a Christian and his use of morality as a club to fight those who did not submit to his domination. On the other hand, Allen resisted these attempts and countered Dr. Mann's questions with equally aggressive questions.

There was no follow-up on this interview because Allen did not return to Dr. Mann's office. Nor did he pursue the idea of the ministry further with any faculty member. Through the student grapevine it was learned that Allen had been dating other girls while he was engaged to Coleen. A number of students commented that Allen wanted to tell everyone what to do but was successful only for short periods of time with some girl who was willing to date him.

Some counselor may uncover the hidden insecurities and feelings of unworthiness which cause Allen to hold the defensive shield of self-righteousness so high.

Vocational Growth in College

Allen could have been used as an example of vocational growth in college except that he gave up his plans for the ministry. In many, many instances young people continue their interest in a church vocation throughout college or make their decision for such work during this time. Students who were consulted about this matter felt that campus religious organizations were very helpful to them, but they seldom mentioned any personal counseling with a director of such organizations.

The problems most frequently mentioned by students in college were: thinking out theology, work as a student pastor or other religious worker, and doubts about the call from God.

Students are not looking for swift, informal, pat answers:

My most serious problem was that of creed—belief. On this problem I found most of those in places of responsibility quite unwilling to discuss matters of religious faith and practice without statements such as "When you get right with God you will see . . . ," by which they meant that I would agree with them.

Some of the deeper problems could not be written in, for they were often unknown to the student himself. But as one student put it, "I just needed someone to talk with who had an idea of what was going on in my mind." A few informal conversations with a counselor may be enjoyable but they do not meet the heartfelt needs of students.

One fourth of the students were seeking someone who could help them with intimate personal conflicts. Over half of them wanted to talk with someone who could give them correct information and advice based on personal experiences. Only one out of five said that he felt no need for counsel in college.

There were several differences in the college needs of students of various denominations. Lutherans and Evangelical United Brethren were the most troubled about the temptation to give up the decision for a church vocation. Baptists were only one-fourth as interested in this as the Lutherans. Evangelical United Brethren had the most doubts about their call from God (30 per cent) and the Disciples the least (8 per cent). Twice as many Lutherans as any other group considered dropping out of college. However, only 2 per cent of the Lutheran students wanted help when thinking over their theology, whereas 34 per cent of the Methodists and 20–27 per cent of other denominations desired such aid. Lutherans had five times more need for a job to help them through college than any other group.

Religious counsel is of exceptional importance in all three of the major problems mentioned by students: "thinking out theology," "work as a student pastor or other religious worker," and "doubts about the call from God." What diverse areas are involved in an effective counseling ministry!

The counselor who would help a student "think out" his theology must strike a balance between two things, the eternal truths of God and the student's own human situation. For example, concern over theological questions may reflect the existence of problems that are basically emotional rather than intellectual. In such a case, the clearest intellectual answers may leave basic needs unmet. The thoughtful counselor will seek to understand each student's needs before he offers easy answers to theological questions.

Even when a student's primary need appears to be intellectual guidance, a good counselor will take time to determine the student's level of understanding before stating dogmatic theological beliefs. Learning in theology, as in other areas, is a step-by-step process. Good theological insight often can be developed only after childhood misconceptions are cleared away. Roughshod handling of a student's inadequate beliefs can produce emotional damage.

The counselor should be gentle not only about what a student believes but about what he does not believe. Respect for the student as a person requires a willingness to listen patiently to his doubts. Honest questions, regardless of how unnecessary they may seem to the counselor, should be given careful answers. The counselor may cherish his own convictions, but he must always remember that each person must arrive at convictions for himself. Good counsel can help another to develop convictions, but it cannot—and does not seek to—force acceptance of the counselor's beliefs. Acceptance must be won, not demanded.

When the counselor recognizes that theological questions are basically emotional, he will seek to deal with them in that light. A student who shows great concern about Paul's teachings on sin and grace may be struggling with the same problem in his own life. He may want to love people and be loved by them, but ever and again the rigid training of his past may rise up to condemn him for such humanity. This dilemma is part of the growth process in many healthy people and is to be distinguished from the unhealthy chronic preoccupation with little sins that used to be called "scrupulosity." Today "scrupulosity" might be called "compulsion."

Such compulsion may appear religiously in a discussion about many small sins, such as throwing gum wrappers on the campus lawn. One student who suffered from this way of thinking rationalized his concern by saying: "I used to worry about my compulsion to pick up paper. Before that I thought I'd be arrested if I threw any down myself. But now I say, 'Oh well, this will give somebody a job picking up paper.'" The underlying, unknown anxiety was made bearable through anxiety about something tangible. But this maneuver was not entirely successful, so the individual worried about his meticulousness. Finally he developed a counterdefense of sloppiness.

Paul knew well the futility of such legalisms from his own experience (Romans 7). The pastor will have it demonstrated to him both through the repetitive self-flagellations of counselees and the failure of any attempts to impose advice or reassurance upon such persons. One woman said to her pastor: "I read a book a friend gave me and tried to think positive thoughts. But then I had another depression and had to take shock treatments. One reason I became so depressed was because I would think negative thoughts and then feel guilty because I was not thinking positive ones."

It is obvious that religious counselors have a major responsibility in helping with problems concerning student pastorates. Unfortunately, many profitable interviews are ruined through the counselor's intoning of such phrases as: "It has been my experience," "Now when I was at First Church . . ." Students made it clear through the 1954 questionnaire that they sought out a professor of religion or pastor because they knew religion from the inside. *Some* concrete statements from experience are invaluable. But the student has his own problems that must be solved in his own way. The counseling is more successful if the *student* is continually saying: "My experience at Crossroads Mission is . . . ," "I have found that . . ."

"Doubts about God" may be the result of many things: a scrupulous conscience, extreme dogmatism, or self-deception about guilt. At times it is the normal result of the shift from externalism in religion to inner faith. A student may tell his pastor: "I just can't believe in religion any more the way I was taught it back at Startown. Now I know what some of those Sunday school teachers are really like." Such knowledge shows that the student is becoming aware of the realities of the world—and of religion. The question is what he will do with his knowledge.

The realistic acceptance of sin within Christianity does not minimize the importance of the problem. The student may doubt God because he rejects the overbearing, unfeeling attitudes of a parent, pastor, or Sunday school teacher. His doubt is often the symptom of a break in the Christian fellowship. As one college student expressed it:

> They were fighting in my church back home. I was disgusted with the way my brother acted. They made him into a fanatic. My Jewish roommate seemed more Christian than some of those church members. I finally got it out of my system by disbelieving everything they had taught me. If it hadn't been for a good chaplain whom I met overseas, I would never have gone into the ministry.

A counseling pastor will not defend institutionalized religion. The book of Acts, the pastoral epistles, or the first three chapters of Revelation demonstrate what the student has just discovered—*that the church is composed of sinners*. Is this young man willing to lay aside his early adolescent idealization of religion and become a mature Christian who is not swayed by every wind of doctrine or scandal? Maturity comes only when he knows that ultimately there is nothing worth boasting about except the Lord (1 Cor. 1:31). The acts of men are imperfect. The church is built upon one perfect act, the sacrifice in love and the resurrection in power of Christ.

Problems in Professional School

If students are already facing personal problems, these difficulties are intensified when they reach the seminary. The need for counsel during an inner personal struggle was mentioned more than anything else by students in seminary. These struggles might be a marital conflict intensified by the fact that the wife works while the husband attends classes, or the sudden death of a parent which leaves the student to care for his mother and sisters, or perhaps rebellion which causes the student to fail courses as an indirect way of revenge upon a father who forced the student to choose the ministry.

The pressure of professional training creates problems and intensifies old ones. "Choosing a field of service" was the second most frequently mentioned problem in seminary. Problems in connection with student church work were third. Students were harassed by the competitive, hurried atmosphere of the larger seminaries. They found it difficult to seek counsel at the very time that their problems were becoming more complex. Many seminary students made suggestions about these difficulties. A representative comment was:

Could we not set up a system of counseling on the campus on a wider scale? So many of us have problems that go untouched by us or a counselor.

I believe that every student should be studied by a counselor before he enters the seminary. I think at least a few people could be weeded out when found to have wrong motives for coming here. It seems hard, but the situation demands it.

In the larger seminaries, students felt frustrated because they did not have personal contact with professors whom they respected. One student wrote: "I believe that if the professors would consider the students their flock or their 'disciples,' they would foster better student relations and turn out more wholesome pastors."

Several answers to these student suggestions have already been devised. One is the varied series of tests now given to matriculating theological students. A major problem is how these tests are to be evaluated and used with the student. When counseling facilities are available to follow up these tests, they may become an asset both to the student and to the school.[2]

The requests for counseling on seminary campuses have been met in several ways. Some schools employ a psychiatrist to be on the campus where students may come to know him. Some will seek therapy; others will be benefited from his presence in a group. A number of seminaries have now found, or are seeking, a professor of pastoral psychology who would have the academic background for both theological teaching and clinical training. Such a professor often finds the majority of problem students sent his way. This is unfortunate for two reasons. First, it creates intolerable pressure when the professor is already carrying a full teaching schedule. Second, it conveys the idea that the psychology professor alone is responsible for student growth and pastoral care.

Actually, the presence of a teacher of pastoral psychology should be the stimulus for *all* the faculty to give more time to students' personal problems and recognize the place of emotional growth in all academic fields. What better opportunity to know a student's emotional health is there than in "practice preaching"?

What subject demands more clinical pastoral education than a biblical instructor's exegesis of the "call," prophecy, or charismatic gifts? An emotionally disturbed student is often noticed in his first semester term papers, a full year before the professor of pastoral psychology usually has him in a class.

An unusual opportunity to help student families with their personal difficulties is the seminary nursery or day school. Skilled workers observe signs of home disturbance in the reactions of a child. At the monthly parents' meeting, general problems of family living are discussed. In addition, the parents of a child with serious behavior problems are seen privately. In both the group and individual sessions student pastors and their wives may learn more effective and healthy ways of living with each other and their children. When he has learned to rule his own household well, the young minister is fit to shepherd one of God's families—a church. Yet how many denominations are so careful about a minister's training that they tremble at Paul's question, "If a man does not know how to manage his own household, how can he care for God's church?" (1 Tim. 3:5).

In conclusion, it must be said that these are the problems as the young people themselves see them and as they are able to write them down or check them on a questionnaire. The great challenge to pastoral counselors is to identify for themselves the great opportunities that are before them in face-to-face contact with young people. New and varied problems and possible solutions for living continually unfold. Each pastor can hope to share the sense of mission expressed by a seminary student: "My prayer is that my life will be dedicated to serving those with whom I work and not withdrawing myself from them."

VIII
Preaching on Church Vocations

Evidence on the direct ways in which a sermon influences a person toward a church vocation is lacking. Ralph Felton's study of 1,573 ministerial students in 1949 listed "sermons of a pastor" as the ninth element or event which influenced them to choose the ministry. Home training, contacts with a pastor, and contemporary world needs were the situations most often mentioned.[1]

The 1954 study at Southern Baptist Theological Seminary revealed that the largest percentage (32 per cent) of Baptist students made their decision public at the close of a sermon by their pastor. Such a large percentage was not true of other denominations. Among Disciples, Presbyterians, Methodists, and Episcopalians it was more customary for the pastor to make an announcement or give notice through the church bulletin.

Despite the lack of extensive evidence, all can agree that the sermon *is* an opportunity to interpret the general call of all men to Christ's service and the definite call to a church vocation. In the sermon, young people can be challenged to dedicate themselves to service within the church, and specific information can be given which will help them in this decision. All this will be a background and supplement to personal counseling regarding their choice.

Church vocations are a part of sermons in various ways: personal examples in the lives of ministers or missionaries may be referred to in various sermons; Christian living is often the sermon theme, and a church vocation may be mentioned as one way to serve God; sermons dealing with religious experience or the theology of inspiration offer opportunity to explain God's call to full-time service; a sermon may be devoted exclusively to recruitment for church vocations, explaining the need, giving information, and challenging young people to definite commitment.

An example of each of these can be considered here to see how they affected different individuals' thinking.

Personal Examples

Ministers or missionaries are often used for illustrative purposes. In preaching on the gospel as the savor of life (Matt. 5:13–16), a pastor gave this example:

It took a simple shoemaker to rescue the savor of the gospel among Baptists. When William Carey preached on the text, "Expect great things from God; attempt great things for God," many were impressed, but the next day they had lost the vision and urged caution in taking any missionary action. Then Carey turned to one of the greatest Baptist preachers of his day, Andrew Fuller, and said, "Is there nothing again going to be done, sir?" Fuller was shaken out of his lethargy, rose to his feet, and with the prestige of his years and learning won the assembly which was skeptical of "that hair-brained enthusiast," Carey.

Who will rescue the savor of the gospel among us today? There are young people with Carey's vision in our congregation. Which of you will accept the challenge to make life zestful and attractive to others through the preaching of the kingdom of God?

It was at the close of this sermon that a young man came before the congregation to state publicly his decision to enter a church vocation. To the pastor he said, "I had already made my decision, but the example you gave in the sermon surely helped."

Serving God

Church vocations may be mentioned as one way to serve God. For instance, if a pastor used one of the chapter headings in Professor Latourette's *The Christian World Mission in Our Day*, "The Eternal Gospel in an Age of Storm," he could bring in full-time kingdom service in this way:

What can we do to set up new moorings for our world today? There are some who will go as missionaries supported by churches. There are many more who will be missionaries even though they are not supported by churches. They will be members of the armed forces in occupied territory, or representatives of commercial or industrial firms of the United States. And just as the natives will watch every move of the young man or woman from "Christian America," so they will read in the newspapers of our activities at home as well. Greed and prejudice here can undermine Christianity a thousand miles away. Unless we lead a life of obedient love to Christ wherever we are—missionary in Africa or storekeeper in America—we shall not overcome the storms of this world.

During the week following this sermon, the pastor who preached it had a conference with a young lady who was trying to decide whether to finish her master's degree for public school teaching or enter a school of religious education. She said, "I liked your sermon about serving God here as well as abroad. I once thought of being a missionary. I thought it was the only real Christian life, but I don't think so any more. I'm pretty sure that however I make up my mind, I can still serve God, teaching in a public school or in a church."

God's Call

Pastors can approach the basic decision for the ministry by choosing God's call as the central theme of a sermon. One of the most complete biblical examples would be Isaiah 6. An outline of such a sermon might include:

Introduction: the contrast between the religion of men, typified by the good King Uzziah, and Isaiah's experience with God which followed his hero's death (Isa. 6:1–3). The experience of Isaiah contained four great thoughts:

I. The sacredness of God (Isa. 6:1).
    a. The power of God (Isa. 6:4, 2:11, 4; Ezek. 22:29–31).
    b. The purity of God (Isa. 6:5, 8–9).

II. The sinfulness of man (Isa. 6:5, 55:8–9).

III. The salvation of man: God judges men only to save them (Isa. 6:6–7; Psalm 51:6–12).

IV. A sense of mission (Isa. 6:8–9).

Conclusion: God is speaking to your heart this morning (Isa. 55:6–7).

At the conclusion of this sermon, Joe, the young person discussed in a previous chapter, told his pastor that it was a help in understanding more fully the nature of God's call.

Although this sermon does outline the elements of personal religious experience with God, it did not give Joe all the help that he needed. He would need to hear additional sermons in which the pastor explains that God speaks to people in many ways. Some people are still waiting for some cataclysmic experience. Despite the warnings of Paul, 1 Corinthians 14, against an emphasis on bizarre experiences, some youths expect to actually hear a voice. Joe could also profit from a sermon distinguishing between the general call to salvation and the call to a particular vocation. It could show the place of the ministry within the Christian fellowship.

Church Vocations

An example of another type of sermon is a discussion of church vocations and a call for commitment to work in organized Christianity. The biblical passages mentioned in a previous chapter are representative of many texts upon which the pastor may build his message.

Many significant facts can be utilized in his preparation. The theology of a Christian calling needs explanation.

Young people also want to know how others have understood and described their decisions for service in the church. Hundreds of stirring examples are available in the biographies and autobiographies of pastors and missionaries.

However, it is not enough just to tell how others have made the decision. In this complex age, with so many responsibilities pressing upon the church worker, the pastor must outline in some detail how interested persons may prepare for service as a pastor, educational director, missionary, or other servant of the church. In some communions no public decision is called for, but there is still a strong tradition among many churches for a definite commitment before the congregation. The sermon, therefore, should include a note of specific commitment, such as: "Some of you young people may not yet be decided. I would be happy to talk with you about this matter in my office following the morning service or at the youth fellowship hour this evening." "Some young people have already talked to me about this matter. Are you willing to make a public stand before the congregation this morning?" If no public commitment is sought, the pastor may say: "Men of old sought the counsel of others when they were struggling with this weighty decision concerning their life's work. Should this not be more true today when so much is required of one who prepares for a church vocation? I will be happy to talk with any of you about this matter before our evening fellowship or at your convenience during the week."

If a display table of literature is provided, it would be well to include some of the literature on church vocations. Some person who will not come to the pastor may take home a pamphlet that will mold his decision for God.

When young people feel God's challenge rising within them, they want to know how to find the will of God. One of the simplest explanations, which then must be filled in from the hearer's own experience, is to say, "I want to hear how you personally understand this, but briefly, let me conclude by saying that finding God's way includes three things: a knowledge of a need, some self-understanding, and then a dedicated willingness to commit the best you have to meet the need as God guides you."

Those members of the congregation who are concerned about their vocational future will appreciate an analysis of personal and educational requirements for the ministry and some explanation of the fact that many different types of church service are open to men and women with different aptitudes and interests. The pastor who emphasizes an ability to get along with people and who is also sympathetic and understanding as he presents the awesome challenge of a life devoted exclusively to organized religion will help to clear up confusion in the minds of many hearers.

111

IX

Pastoral Care of Candidates for the Ministry

Like couples preparing for marriage, young people preparing for a church vocation do not see all implications of their intentions at once. Their major problems change from time to time; there are difficulties at the time of the decision and commitment, during college years, and in a different fashion in the seminary. Financing an education is a pressing problem in the beginning, as is the burden of the long preparation lying ahead. The student in college faces new problems as a student pastor or in the confusions that come as he tries to think out his own theology. By the time of seminary training, candidates are concerned about the choice of a specific field of service and about how they can manage until graduation.

The present investigation makes it clear that candidates for church vocations have problems at every stage in their development. They need, and often ask for, pastoral care in each of these stages. Consideration of some of the ways in which a pastor may extend the care of his church to young people from the time of their vocational decision through their formal education may help him to give intelligent and helpful guidance. A pastor might, at different times, use all of these methods; he might use only one.

Sermons have already been discussed; the great aid that preaching can give to counseling has been pointed out. Candidates for the ministry are stimulated by hearing sermons that help them to think out their own theology and that are models of what their future sermons should be. The value of sermons with specific objectives cannot be overemphasized. A recurring theme of life dedication may run through the preaching ministry like the refrain repeated through a symphony.

Discussion groups and retreats are some of the most neglected resources. Only 15 per cent of fifteen hundred students said that they were helped with their problems through group conferences with a professional church worker.

As an example of topics for group discussions, there are the pamphlets of Dr. John Oliver Nelson (obtainable from the Commission on the Ministry, 297 Fourth Avenue, New York 10, New York): "How About My Career Choice?" "Can the Church Offer Me a Career?" "Why Have Ministers?"

Additional topics for discussion may be found in the pamphlet series of The Student Volunteer Movement (156 Fifth Avenue, New York 10, New York):

"Why Force My Religion on Others?"
"Why Not Our Own Backyard First?"
"Isn't the Missionary Job Already Done?"
"Aren't Missions a Form of Western Imperialism?"

"Do Missions Serve Modern Needs in Up-to-Date
Ways?"

"Can a Divided Church Do the Missionary Job?"

"Can Christianity Out-Perform Communism?"

"How Do I Know I'm Called?"

Life-Service Bands provide a way in which several
young people in one church or locality who have decided for a church vocation can meet weekly or monthly
for fellowship and discussion of mutual problems. In
larger churches there may be a sizable group with
a well-developed program. In smaller communities
young people from various churches may meet together
for this common purpose. The pastor, or pastors, can
meet with them to answer questions, to supply them
with definite materials on church vocations, and to ar-
range for persons in various types of church vocations
to come before them.

Once the youth is in college, he can find the value
of campus religious organizations in meeting those same
needs. Seminary students said that these organizations
helped them in the cultivation of their devotional life,
in providing experience as a leader of religious activities, and in feeling at ease with a group.

Supervised church work is another valuable aid. Pastors may take it for granted that the candidate will
work in the church, but such an assumption misses a
valuable opportunity to teach young people through experience. Although candidates should not be made the
"beasts of burden" in routine jobs which no one else
will take, nor made to stand out apart from other young

people, the pastor can make it clear to them in private that they are to feel free to explore the inner workings of the church and to talk with him about them at any time.

After Joe had made his decision for a church vocation public, he continued to work in his college religious group and joined a college ministers' association. When he came home for the summer, he suggested to the pastor that the young people's Sunday school class begin some mission project. He had already recruited a friend as musician. Joe and the pastor went over a recent church census and selected an unchurched area where Sunday school work could begin, then presented the idea to the deacons and secured the sponsorship of the church for this mission work.

Joe was appointed director of the work with the understanding that the mission offering would help pay his week-end travel expenses from a neighboring college in the fall. His Sunday school class provided teachers; the church provided the literature and rented the recreation building in the housing project where the Sunday school was started. Joe became thoroughly acquainted with the practical problems of religious education and pastoral visitation. He talked many of these problems over with the pastor.

After one year the church sponsored a revival in the mission Sunday school. Those who made a profession of faith were enrolled in the parent church, just as they had been carried previously on the church Sunday school rolls. When adults in the area began to attend and several were enlisted as Sunday school teachers after joining the parent church, Joe asked for the privilege of starting his own church service. The church voted to license him to preach upon recommendation from the pastor and deacons.

Meanwhile, some of the young people who taught in the mission Sunday school became interested in a church vocation. They led the entire Sunday school of the parent church to adopt a "Christian service project" for each class. These young people repeated the same steps Joe had taken, consulting the pastor about each stage of their decision as it affected the church or their future vocation. Several of them made routine calls with the pastor and attended funerals with him.

The advantages of supervised church work are obvious. The church is a part of all that the young person does, and he is a part of its fellowship. The candidate for a church vocation is not distinguished from other dedicated young people except that this work is also practical experience for his future vocation. The entire church benefits from such activity, and seeds of interest are sown in other hearts through a living witness in the church. Young people have a reason for consulting their pastor as one who can advise them in the practical affairs of the church. They are constantly encouraged to stand on their own judgments as he coaches them in their professional experiences.

Academic preparation may require both advice and direct assistance from the pastor. Financing an education was more of a problem among those questioned in 1956 (36 per cent) than deciding what school to attend (20 per cent). Evidence is not available as to what part pastors took in helping students finance their education. It is known that many directors of college guidance programs did not recommend one specific seminary to students. Instead, the majority recommended various institutions that would meet the needs of particular students.[1]

Pastors can be of specific assistance in securing college and seminary catalogs and showing from the seminary catalogs the recommendations for college preparation. Since many persons cannot understand a catalog, the pastor will do well to interpret it for the student. Students are also reassured when the pastor tells them that he knows this professor or that another is outstanding in his field.

Although college students do not write many letters to pastors, they do appreciate occasional letters from their pastors. Students are sometimes bitter because the pastor who pleaded almost in tears for volunteers for a church vocation extolled their decision but never contacted them again. As one seminary student wrote: "He treated me like a statistic. He made sure that the church reported an additional decision for Christian service, but he never paid any attention to me again."

Farsighted pastors will set aside time during college holidays or during summer vacations to talk with students, especially those interested in a church vocation. This is their time to express their doubts, raise questions about theology, and talk about love affairs or dreams of future efforts by which they may revitalize the church.

Introducing young people to denominational life is essential. Pastors may be surprised at the ignorance of candidates for church vocations concerning the organization and objectives of their denomination. Even if the candidate knows one section of the work, or sees the whole on paper, he still needs to meet leaders, attend meetings, and listen to ministerial lobby conversations, all of which reveal the inner life of a denomination.

Young people can be taken by the pastor to ministerial associations, regional meetings, or an occasional national conference. He can recommend that the church send young candidates to such meetings. They may pay more attention to the formal proceedings than the pastor does! This is a vital time for pastors to show the denomination to young people from a mature point of view. Often this will be a time of disillusionment when the candidate sees the gap between Christian theory and ecclesiastical practice. He needs a pastor who will patiently hear him explode about inconsistency and compromise, yet be an informed listener who can point out ways by which these problems can be met.

Preparation for licensing or ordination requires careful pastoral care. At these times the young candidate can feel the significance of the ministry as it is mediated to him by a group of concerned pastors and laymen. Yet often these events mark the beginning of separations, as some candidate comes ill-prepared to state his convictions or finds that he is caught in the cross fire between opposing theological factions. The pastor can be a great aid by telling the candidate what is expected of him in terms of information and how he may be straightforward in meeting the leading questions that a hostile person may ask him.

Since procedures for licensing and ordination differ among denominations, each pastor will adopt different methods in the care of his young charges. However, there is some information common to all communions.

First, there are the great passages on the pastoral office found in 1 Timothy 3:1-7, Titus 1:5-9, and 1 Peter 5:1-4. The personal qualifications of the pastor set forth therein are specific. The young man who takes them to heart will find them vividly illustrated in his later experience.

Second, there must be some interpretation of what the word "minister" signifies to people. Whether his denomination stresses the sacraments or not, the clergyman is a representative of God. The candidate needs careful instruction concerning the ways by which his conduct and attitudes may reflect credit upon his Lord. Jeremiah and Ezekiel have much to say about true and false prophets. Paul states his convictions in 2 Corinthians 1:12-4:18. God makes his appeal through his ambassadors upon earth (2 Cor. 5:20).

The pastor is also a reminder of the life of Jesus. Experienced ministers can tell young men how the simple act of stooping down to shake hands with little children after church is a living reminder of Christ. Perhaps less visibly, one set apart for the upbuilding of the kingdom is an instrument of the Holy Spirit. New ministers may be anxious to teach by word of mouth all they learned in seminary lectures. College students may be fearful lest they forget all they hope to learn in seminary. But the mature minister can remind them that spiritual communication is like deep water. A man of understanding can draw it out more easily by his unspoken attitudes rather than by his much speaking.

The Holy Spirit teaches men in the crises of life. Once received, his lesson is known to all who have suffered in like fashion from humiliation, heartbreak, or bereavement. As one veteran pastor told a seminary teacher, "Young Johnson will make a fine minister some day, but his heart has never been broken. He pushes people out of his way and does not enter into their sorrow. I cannot tell him this, for he does not know what he lacks. But I pray that I may be close enough to him when a crisis comes that I can comfort him with the knowledge that now his real understanding of people has begun."

Each minister represents his own church, his own denomination. This fact does not detract from his universal witness as a man of God; it establishes certain patterns of behavior with members of his congregation. Thus, one patient in a mental hospital asked the chaplain during a ward visit if he were looking for "joiners." Her church was a gathered community, a group who professed faith in Christ after they were old enough to take responsibility for such action. Another patient asked for communion at her bedside. Her church was an encompassing community, one that went out to the individual with the sacraments.

As a representative of one communion, every prospective minister needs instruction in the beliefs of his denomination. Care must be exercised to see that this is not mere rote memory or the parroting of phrases to pass an examination. The inner reservations of each candidate will come to the surface only when the pastor takes time to ask how particular doctrines apply in this young man's personal experience.

A final obligation of the counselor of candidates is to present an over-all perspective of the pastoral office. When young men have worked closely with their pastor in church duties, much of this will already be known. But each prospective minister needs some philosophy, some set of vocational goals, to guide him through the maze of theological education. Professors do not always take time to relate their particular subject to the total task of the minister or even to other courses in the seminary curriculum.[2] The young man who has had some previous instruction "in the field" will be better prepared for the rigors of first-year courses that seem only distantly related to the saving of souls or the efficient handling of multitudinous details of church organization.

A glorious moment comes to all when the pastor has completed this instruction and has seen his young charge emerge from a council meeting with the praises of his elders lifting up his heart. But the relationship of pastor to student is not ended. In years ahead there will be times of stress when each man will return to the one who taught him for counsel concerning a marital heartbreak, a personal tragedy, a crucial change of pastorates.

The words of John Henry Jowett well express the charge of every pastor to those he has shepherded toward a church vocation:

My brethren, you are going forth in a big world to confront big things. There is "the pestilence that walketh in darkness," and there is "the destruction that wasteth at noonday." There is success and there is failure, and there is sin and sorrow and death. And of all pathetic plights surely the most pathetic is that of a minister moving about this grim field of varied necessity, professing to be a physician, but carrying in his wallet no balms, no cordials, no caustics to meet the clamant needs of men. But of all privileged callings surely the most privileged is that of Greatheart facing the highways of life, carrying with him all that is needed by fainting, bruised and broken pilgrims, perfectly confident in Him "Whom he has believed." Brethren, your calling is very holy. Your work is very difficult. Your Savior is very mighty. And the joy of the Lord will be your strength.[3]

Notes

CHAPTER I

1. Washington Gladden, *Recollections* (Boston: Houghton Mifflin Co., 1909), pp. 324–26.

2. Charles F. Kemp, *Physicians of the Soul* (New York: The Macmillan Co., 1950), p. 120.

3. American and Southern Baptists, Disciples of Christ, Episcopal, Evangelical United Brethren, Missouri Synod Lutheran, Methodist, and Southern Presbyterian.

4. As quoted in Austin K. DeBlois and Lemuel C. Barnes, *John Mason Peck and One Hundred Years of Home Missions, 1817–1917* (New York: American Baptist Home Mission Society, 1917), p. 61; used by permission.

5. All biblical quotations are from the Revised Standard Version.

6. Richard Baxter, *The Reformed Pastor* (London: Epworth Press, 1939), p. 79; used by permission.

7. Dr. George Arbaugh, "Guiding Men Out of the Ministry and In," *Lutheran Church Quarterly,* XVII (1943), 239; used by permission.

CHAPTER II

1. Arbaugh, *op. cit.,* p. 239.

2. A general discussion of the differences between healthy and unhealthy religion is found in Wayne E. Oates, *Religious Factors in Mental Illness* (New York: Association Press, 1955), chapter 4.

3. Harry Emerson Fosdick, *Living Under Tension* (New York: Harper & Brothers, 1941), p. 187; used by permission.

CHAPTER III

1. Baxter, *op. cit.,* pp. 75–76.
2. *Ibid.,* p. 79.

CHAPTER IV

1. Mr. George Stoll, Paul's Workshop, 241 East Walnut Street, Louisville 2, Kentucky. *Laymen at Work* is the story of the Louisville Committee, told by George Stoll and Albert Meiburg.
2. Martin Luther, *Works of Martin Luther* (Philadelphia: Muhlenberg Press, 1915), I, 179.
3. John Calvin, *Institutes of the Christian Religion* (Edinburgh: Edinburgh Printing Co., 1846), IV, 68–71, 83.
4. Baxter, *op. cit.,* p. 131.
5. As quoted in E. D. Jones, *The Royalty of the Pulpit* (New York: Harper & Brothers, 1951), p. 332; used by permission.

CHAPTER VI

1. Simon Doniger (ed.), "Readers' Forum," *Pastoral Psychology,* VI (Nov., 1955), 57–58; used by permission.
2. *Ibid.,* p. 59.
3. Hugh Hartshorne and Milton Froyd, *Theological Education in the Northern Baptist Convention* (Philadelphia: Judson Press, 1945), p. 168.
4. *Grace Abounding to the Chief of Sinners* (Philadelphia: American Baptist Publication Society, 1852), pp. 108–109.
5. P. W. James, *George Truett* (New York: The Macmillan Co., 1945), p. 26; used by permission.
6. Gladden, *op. cit.,* pp. 63, 86.
7. Alexander Allen, *Phillips Brooks* (New York: E. D. Sutton Co., 1907), p. 37.
8. Robert Philip, *Life and Times of the Reverend*

George Whitefield, M.A. (London: George Virtue, 1842),
pp. 11–12.

9. Edwin Holt Hughes, *I Was Made a Minister* (New
York: Abingdon-Cokesbury, 1943), pp. 1–2; used by permission.

10. Mrs. Sam Jones, *Life and Sayings of Sam Jones* (At-
lanta: Franklin-Turner Co., 1906), p. 54.

11. Paxton Hibben, *Henry Ward Beecher: an American
Portrait* (New York: George H. Doran Company, 1927),
p. 29.

12. *Ibid.,* p. 333.

13. George A. Smith, *Life of Henry Drummond* (New
York: Hodder and Stroughton, 1898), pp. 39–40, 79.

14. Winston C. Crawley, "The Call to Foreign Missions
Among Southern Baptists" (Doctoral dissertation, Southern
Baptist Theological Seminary, 1947), pp. 132–135; used by
permission.

15. Philip Alaimo, "Factors Influencing Ministers' Vocational Choice" (Master's thesis, Northwestern University,
1940), p. 81.

16. Abbott Herman, *Motivating Factors Entering into the
Choice of the Ministry* (Chicago: University of Chicago
Libraries, 1932), pp. 9 ff.

17. Robert Smith, "Personality and Cultural Factors Af-
fecting the Religion of One Hundred and Forty Divinity
Students," *Religious Education,* XLIII No. 1 (1948), p. 111.

CHAPTER VII

1. A penetrating group of prayers for pastors are those of
Dr. George Redding, *The Southwell Litany* (Cincinnati:
Forward Movement Publications, n.d.).

2. For further discussion of this issue, see Elmer Million,
"Psychological Testing in the Seminaries," *Bulletin of the
American Association of Theological Schools,* No. 21 (1954),
85–99.

CHAPTER VIII

1. *New Ministers* (Madison, New Jersey: Drew Theological Seminary, 1949) , p. 10.

CHAPTER IX

1. Samuel Southard, "College Counseling Regarding Church Vocations," *Southern Baptist Educator,* XVIII (May, 1954) , 11.

2. H. Richard Niebuhr, *The Purpose of the Church and Its Ministry* (New York: Harper & Brothers, 1956) , p. 99.

3. Jones, *op. cit.,* p. 82.